T0311912

"In this compact volume on culture and governance in China and East Asia, Hong Hai covers a wide field simply and succinctly. It is eminently readable and provides the best single short introduction to the region that I have come across. He paints in broad strokes covering a wide landscape with surprising depth. For some parts, he sketches interesting details which enhance and strengthen the overall presentation.

It is remarkable how Hong Hai is able to explain diverse subjects – from the philosophy of Confucianism, Taoism, Buddhism to the leadership styles of Mao Tse-Tung, Deng Xiaoping and Lee Kuan Yew, to the success of companies like China's Alibaba, Japan's Toyota, Korea's Samsung and Hong Kong's Esquel, to recent scandals involving foreigners brought into companies like Olympus and Nissan – in a way which make them all cohere and explicable against the history and culture of the chopsticks peoples.

For those wishing to understand more deeply the backdrop of China's and East Asia's response to the actions of the Trump Administration, this quick read can be very helpful."

– **George Yeo**, *Chairman, Kerry Logistics Network and Visiting Scholar, Lee Kuan Yew School of Public Policy, National University of Singapore. Mr Yeo served with distinction in the Singapore government cabinet, holding among others the key posts of Minister for Foreign Affairs and Minister for Trade and Industry.*

"Drawing on a wealth of research and years of experience in academia, business, and politics, Professor Hong Hai persuasively argues for the importance of culture in East Asia. He not only shows how culture affects the workings of economic and political organizations: he also shows how modernized interpretations of traditional values can make those organizations work better in the future."

– **Daniel A. Bell**, *Dean of the School of Political Science and Public Administration at Shandong University and Professor at Tsinghua University; author of* The China Model.

"The 21st century will be the Asian century. Asia's success has been driven by a dynamic fusion of the best from the East and the West. We know well how the West transformed the world. We know little about how Asia's resurgence was driven by its own cultures and values.

In this volume, Hong Hai, a deep student of Asian history and culture, has distilled well the key elements of Asian cultures and shown how they relate to successful corporate practices as well as state governance in dynamic Asian economies. Those who want to get a glimpse of the Asian century should dive into this book."

– **Kishore Mahbubani**, *Distinguished Fellow, Asia Research Institute, National University of Singapore, and author of* Has the West Lost It? *Professor Mahbubani previously served as Dean of the Lee Kuan Yew School of Public Policy and has written and lectured extensively on Asian affairs and China–US relations.*

"In this book Professor Hong has presented us with a deft and gentle interrogation of authoritarian regimes across East Asia, from the largest (China) to the very smallest (Singapore). He has consciously adopted the perspective of a cultural and political insider and in doing so he has brought a different quality to that of an overt critic and cultural outsider like myself. Those looking for the rhetorical flourish that delivers a fatal wound to an opponent will be disappointed, but if you want to read an empathetic interrogation of the shortfalls in East Asian authoritarian governance – argued mostly in terms of its own goals and ideological rationales – then you should be well pleased with this offering."

– **Michael Barr**, *Associate Professor of International Relations, College of Business, Government and Law, Flinders University; Associate Editor,* Asian Studies Review *and author of* Singapore: A Modern History *(2019). Professor Barr has written extensively on Singapore politics and authored a much-cited political biography of Lee Kuan Yew.*

"Increasingly there is realization that culture has a profound effect on the success or failure of nations and companies. In recent history, liberal democracy survived and appeared to have worked best among the different options of governance but is starting to see decline all over the world. China and East Asian nations are re-adopting Confucianism. Hong Hai has analysed examples of how Confucian culture has led to successful governance of countries where a majority are oriental people. An excellent read to understand what is happening the world over."

– **Inderjit Singh**, *Chairman, NTU Innovation Centre and former Member of Parliament, Singapore.*

"Covering China, Japan, South Korea and Singapore, he muses over the decisive influence of traditional cultures on corporate behaviour and the governance of states. Especially interesting is his argument that Confucian values still resonate in many 21st-century East Asian countries. He also explores the ideal of a 'meritocratic democracy' in these countries while cognisant of the reality of authoritarian tendencies in their governance. Hong Hai writes: 'It is important for authoritarian governance *not* to have a cruel edge, and for the people in such regimes to realize that there are orderly means to remove a bad leader.' This is indeed a tantalizing thought and a good prescription for all 'emperors,' states, societies and firms, Confucian or otherwise."

– **Lam Peng Er**, *Senior Research Fellow, East Asian Institute, National University of Singapore. Dr Lam is a specialist in Japanese politics and society, and has also written extensively on Singapore history and politics.*

"The book contains the distilled experiences of the author who has had a distinguished career in politics, academia and the corporate world. Taking a broad sweep of the business practices and state governance in China, Japan, South Korea and Singapore, he offers insights through the lens of Confucianism, Daoism and their national histories. The gem of the book is the discussion of the novel concept of meritocratic democracy which draws on the best talents to run the country rather than those who are popular with the masses. Such democracies tend toward benevolent authoritarianism but do not always enjoy universal suffrage; some have been successful and merit study."

– **Michael Heng**, *former professor of management and author of*
The Great Recession: History, Ideology, Hubris and Nemesis.

"In light of China's remarkable rise and the recent seeming dysfunction of Western liberal democracies, the debate on governance has assumed ever greater import. Specifically, does China have political wisdom to share with the West? Is Confucian governance workable only in its land of origin or can it be applied universally? Hong Hai draws from his broad training and experience in economics, philosophy, politics and business to shed light on the question of whether governance is culture- and history-dependent. Based on a successful course he taught at Nanyang Technological University, Hong Hai's book is rich with insights on Confucian virtue and its impact on corporate and state governance in Asia. It is a must read for academics, businespeople and policymakers facing a changing world order."

– **Michael Tai**, *Professor of East Asian Studies at the Beijing Institute of Technology in Zhuhai and Fellow of the Royal Asiatic Society of Great Britain and Ireland; author of* US–China Relations in the Twenty-First Century:
A Question of Trust.

"In these troubled times of bitter rivalry among superpowers and questionable corporate and political governance practices, and with the advent of artificial intelligence and 5G communications, Hong Hai's new book evokes Dickensian characterization. It seems to be the best of times, the worst of times, the age of wisdom, of foolishness, of belief, and of incredulity. Hong Hai painstakingly reflects on cultural history in search of a moral vision to illuminate pitfalls in corporate and political governance. He challenges the false dichotomy between democracy and the authoritarian state as often purveyed by the Western media. With increasingly dysfunctional liberal democracies in the West as the backdrop, he explores how 'meritocratic democracy' may be a viable alternative. His arduous search for a secure and hospitable foundation for governance is very commendable."

– **Chua Lee Beng**, *Educational Consultant, was a faculty member of Dartmouth College and the Harvard Graduate School of Education.*

THE RULE OF CULTURE

Culture has an abiding influence on the way countries and business corporations are governed. This book introduces the reader to the deep philosophies that drive corporations and governments in East Asia, from China through Japan and South Korea to Singapore. With sparkling clarity and spiced with anecdotes and case studies, it depicts how respect for cultures can lead to spectacular success, or the lack of it to failure. Confucian practices such as *guanxi* in Chinese society, the benevolent culture of *entity firms* in Japan, and patriarchal *chaebols* in South Korea are analyzed with examples like Esquel, Nissan, and Samsung. A delightful chapter on Daoism shows how it drives Jack Ma's Alibaba.com.

In the governance of nations, the author reinforces Burke's dictum that systems of government must be consonant with traditional cultures, and he calls out misguided attempts by the West to foist liberal democracies on civilizations in the East where respect for authority and communitarian values come before individual interest. The author advances the novel concept of the *meritocratic democracy* in which leaders are chosen not by electoral popularity but by proven ability. In a thought-provoking concluding chapter, he evaluates prospective constitutional changes in China that would enshrine meritocratic democracy as an alternative to liberal democracies that have turned dysfunctional in many Western nations.

Hong Hai was Professor and Dean of the College of Business at Nanyang Technological University, where he is now Adjunct Professor. He has been a Member of the Singapore Parliament and chief executive of Haw Par Corporation, and published in economics, philosophy, and Chinese history.

Routledge Contemporary Corporate Governance

The *Routledge Contemporary Corporate Governance* Series aims to provide an authoritative, thought-provoking and well-balanced series of textbooks in the rapidly emerging field of corporate governance. The corporate governance literature traditionally has been scattered in the finance, economics, accounting, law and management literature. However the international controversy now associated with corporate governance has focused considerable attention on this subject and raised its profile immeasurably. Government, financial institutions, corporations and academics have become deeply involved in tackling the dilemmas of corporate governance due to widespread public concerns.

The *Routledge Contemporary Corporate Governance* Series will make a significant impact in this emerging field: defining and illuminating problems; going beyond the official emphasis on regulation and procedures to understand the behaviour of executives, boards, and corporations; analysing the wider impact and relationships involved in corporate governance. Issues that will be covered in this series include:

- Exploring the impact of the globalisation of corporate governance
- Assessing ongoing contest between shareholder/stakeholder values
- Examining how corporate governance values determine corporate objectives
- Analysing how financial interests have overwhelmed corporate governance
- Investigating the discourse of corporate governance
- Considering the imperative of sustainability in corporate governance
- Addressing the contemporary crises in corporate governance and how they might be resolved

Series Editor:

Thomas Clarke, Professor of Corporate Governance, University of Technology Sydney, Australia

Editorial Board:

Professor Bernard Taylor, Executive Director of the Centre for Board Effectiveness, Henley Management College, UK

Dr David Wheeler, Erivan K Haub Professor of Business and Sustainability, Schulich School of Business, York University, Canada

Professor Esther Solomon, Graduate School of Business, Fordham University, New York, USA

Professor Jean-Francois Chanlat, CREPA, Director of Executive MBA, Université Paris IX Dauphine, France

The Rule of Culture
Corporate and State Governance in China and East Asia
Hong Hai

For more information about this series, please visit www.routledge.com/series/RCCG

THE RULE OF CULTURE

Corporate and State Governance
in China and East Asia

Hong Hai

LONDON AND NEW YORK

First published 2020
by Routledge
2 Park Square, Milton Park, Abingdon, Oxon OX14 4RN

and by Routledge
52 Vanderbilt Avenue, New York, NY 10017

Routledge is an imprint of the Taylor & Francis Group, an informa business

© 2020 Hong Hai

British Library Cataloguing-in-Publication Data
A catalogue record for this book is available from the British Library

Library of Congress Cataloging-in-Publication Data
Names: Hong, Hai, 1943– author.
Title: The rule of culture : corporate and state governance in China and
    East Asia / Hong Hai.
Description: Abingdon, Oxon ; New York, NY : Routledge, 2020. |
    Includes bibliographical references and index.
Identifiers: LCCN 2019035537 (print) | LCCN 2019035538 (ebook) |
    ISBN 9780367132934 (hardback) | ISBN 9780367132941 (paperback) |
    ISBN 9780429025730 (ebook)
Subjects: LCSH: Management—East Asia. | Corporate culture—East Asia. |
    Corporate governance—East Asia. | Culture. | East Asia—Civilization. |
    East Asia—Politics and government.
Classification: LCC HD70.E22 H66 2020 (print) | LCC HD70.E22 (ebook) |
    DDC 658.0095—dc23
LC record available at https://lccn.loc.gov/2019035537
LC ebook record available at https://lccn.loc.gov/2019035538

ISBN: 978-0-367-13293-4 (hbk)
ISBN: 978-0-367-13294-1 (pbk)
ISBN: 978-0-429-02573-0 (ebk)

Typeset in Bembo
by Apex CoVantage, LLC

CONTENTS

FIGURES

FOREWORD

It is hard to disagree with the opening line of this book's introductory chapter: "Culture has an abiding influence on the way countries and business corporations are governed." The author, Professor Hong Hai, sets out in subsequent chapters to discuss how ancient East Asian philosophies and/or religions continue to influence the way four East Asian countries are governed and their corporations managed today: Confucianism and Daoism in China; Confucianism and Shinto-Buddhism in Japan; Confucianism, Buddhism, and Shamanism in South Korea; and Confucianism in Singapore.

Professor Hong's background and experience as corporate chief executive, business school professor and dean, and Member of the Singapore Parliament make him ideally suited to write such a book. More significantly, the work is, to quote him, a reflection of "a deep interest in culture," which has led him, "years after completing graduate work in economics, to study and research philosophy, Chinese literature, and East Asian history."

The issues raised by Professor Hong in his book are very important, and resonate deeply with contemporary debates on economic development, political systems, and the international world order. In his keynote speech at the Shangri-la Dialogue in June 2019, the prime minister of Singapore, Lee Hsien Loong, commented on the observation that the United States is a young country that wants everyone to be like it.

> To expect every country to adopt the same cultural values and political system is neither reasonable nor realistic. In fact, humankind's diversity is its strength. There is much we can learn from one another, from the differences in our values, perspectives, systems and policies. The story of humankind's progress has been one of exchange of ideas, and continuous learning and adaptation.

In his chapters on the countries, Professor Hong is most confident and authoritative on Singapore. While not wholly uncritical, he writes approvingly of Singapore's "meritocratic democracy." More generally, he postulates that the influence of traditional values – particularly Confucianism – on the four East Asian countries have been positive. They have brought about social stability, effective governance, and, possibly, economic development. Whatever authoritarian tendency, in the mild form, has resulted, it has been worth the loss of some personal freedoms. A trained academic, Professor Hong is aware that correlation is not necessarily causation and that many other factors operate in real time. He is also cognizant of increasing Western cultural influence, especially in Singapore and especially among Millennials.

Professor Hong has written a very good and highly readable introduction to a large, complex, and important area. This book should whet the appetite of those eager to know more about how culture influences organizational design and decision-making in governments and corporations. It is inevitable, given its scope and ambition, that this concise volume on the influence of culture on public policy or corporate decision-making can only touch on most of the subjects covered lightly and obliquely. Thus the book could be a rich source of topics for research projects and in-depth exploration by experts from different disciplines working in teams, with the aim of rigorously probing the questions and matters it has raised.

Dr Teh Kok Peng
Chairman, East Asia Institute and Senior Adviser,
China International Capital Corporation.

PREFACE

East Asian cultures are immensely rich and varied in texture. They draw on deep roots of ancient civilizations that have seen empires rise and fall, whose great thinkers engaged in vigorous debates over the nature of man and the kind of socio-political systems that would govern societies for harmony and economic security.

These cultures remain importantly relevant today, and quietly dictate national and corporate values, hence the title of this book, *The Rule of Culture*. One can easily lose sight of this reality when our linguistic sensibilities are daily assaulted by lax and insensitive use of value-loaded terms like "authoritarianism," "freedom," and "democracy." These words have meanings that vary as widely as the cultures that prevail in different parts of the world.

In the business world, corporate governance is equally influenced by culture. As a result, firms in the East are generally accountable to many stakeholders in various segments of society, in contrast to Western firms focussed on maximizing shareholder wealth.

In this book I have drawn on the rich literature on corporate and state governance and related them to the success, failures, and travails of nations and business corporations alike in the historically rich East Asian region. The book is an outgrowth and expansion of a decade of lectures to succeeding cohorts of international mid-career graduate students selected from civil services, non-government organizations, and private enterprises in a one-year intensive Master's programme focussing on leadership and management.

I would like to gratefully acknowledge the advice of Chua Lee Beng, Lam Peng Er, and Michael Tai, who made very insightful suggestions for improving various parts of the manuscript. However, all views expressed in the book are solely my responsibility. I also thank the many reviewers for their valuable comments, and Teh Kok Peng, Chairman of the East Asia Institute, for writing the Foreword.

Finally, I would like to thank the staff at Routledge, in particular Lam Yong Ling and Samantha Phua, for their tireless efforts in the editing and production of the book, Elaine Koh for the indispensable help going through the manuscript and compiling pictures and illustrations, and Sharon Loo for meticulous copy editing.

The book is dedicated to my late wife, Nancie.

Hong Hai
17 July 2019
Singapore

INTRODUCTION

Culture has an abiding influence on the way countries and business corporations are governed.

Confucian culture has been the state ideology for some two thousand years in imperial China since the Han dynasty. It was briefly sidelined by Marxist thought after the 1949 Chinese Revolution, and attacked during the Cultural Revolution of 1966–1976. But even during those dark days of neglect or repression, Confucianism continued to be deeply embedded in the Chinese language, family traditions, and social values. It has been reasserting itself in recent years following President Xi Jinping's initiative to revive it in 2014.

Confucianism is seriously put forward as the philosophical basis for a new constitution in China. This proposed constitution aims to enshrine, for the people, a system of governance in which the Confucian ideal of a benevolent and sagacious ruling class would be selected through a meritocratic process.

Daoism (Taoism), with its subtle ability to navigate between contradictions and find "Golden Mean" solutions to complex governance issues, has been the fount of Chinese wisdom, much in the same way that Confucianism has been the bedrock of Chinese ethics. After the May Fourth Movement in 1919, freedom of the individual and human rights, cast in Western terms, has had seductive effects on the political values of Chinese youths. But even after a hundred years, it has not taken root in China. Attempts to explain this away by blaming state repression and authoritarianism, however, do not resonate with a deeper understanding of Chinese culture.

The modern political institutions of Japan, South Korea, and Singapore were historically imported from the West.

The Meiji restoration ushered Western influence into Japan, and a leading Japanese intellectual even urged *Datsu-A Ron* ("Goodbye Asia") to embrace the West.[1] The country would go on to make a disastrous turn toward Western-style militant imperialism, which would ultimately end in defeat in World War II. After the war, a liberal democratic system was put in place, although Confucian cultural roots remain a significant influence. It may account for the one-party dominant legislature in most of Japan's post-war history, and explain the current revival of interest in the Confucian capitalism of the charismatic thinker-industrialist Shibusawa Eiichi from the Meiji era.

South Korea evolved toward a liberal democracy after the Korean War and a period of military dictatorship. But her politics suffers from the pernicious influence of Confucian patriarchs of corporate giants, raising doubts that liberal democracy can truly take root in a nation with Confucian cultural genes.

Singapore inherited from her British colonial master the trappings of the Westminster parliamentary democracy. But soon after independence, her founding fathers, led by visionary statesman Lee Kuan Yew, gained control of the institutions of liberal democracy and practised a benevolent form of authoritarian governance guided by Confucian political ideology. The result was an economic miracle and Singapore's transformation into an East Asian state admired in the West.

Corporate governance

In Chinese businesses, corporate governance exists within a framework of family values, respect for authority and hierarchy, and relationship networks. These can play a positive management and social role if there are sufficient institutional safeguards preventing these relationships and connections (*guanxi*) from lapsing into corruption.

Traditional values play similar roles in the business firms of many East Asian economies. In Japan, communitarian values and benevolence toward a large variety of stakeholders – which include employees, customers, and suppliers – form the cultural foundation of the traditional *entity* firm. This is distinct from Western firms that regard the interests of the shareholders as supreme. An entity firm seeks not just to benefit its shareholders but also various other stakeholders and the community in which the firm operates.

In South Korea's powerful conglomerates (*chaebols*), family members control shareholdings and dominate the upper echelons of management. Corruption appears endemic, with frequent corporate scandals involving state officials at high levels. Yet the economy still ranks among the most successful in Asia.

Culture and governance themes in the book

The book begins with a brief introduction to the cultural history of China, followed by an examination of Confucianism and its pervasive influence on state as well as corporate governance (Chapters 1 and 2). My interpretation of the principal precepts of Confucianism would not please the scholar of Confucian thought. Instead of comprehensively presenting the rich and complex rubric of Confucian ethics as it has evolved through the centuries, I have selected aspects of it that relate readily to corporate and state governance in a simple and direct way. In this regard, I have leaned heavily on the writings of Fei Xiaotong, an early twentieth-century sociologist who researched family and social relations in rural China (Chapter 3).

Through case studies of modern corporations like Esquel, Daqian, and CP Pokphand, we will observe how family values and Confucian ethical relationships can work well for corporations that leverage their positive attributes. Practices like *guanxi* and corporate social responsibility are best understood in the framework of Confucian morals rather than business strategies.

Daoism has a longer history and an almost equal claim to Confucianism as the dominant cultural influence in China (Chapter 4). It exerts its influence in fluid and subtle ways, guiding national and corporate leaders to comfortably live with contradictions. These contradictions often arise when legal practices and moral considerations come into mutual conflict. When they do, it is necessary to compromise and seek harmony through a middle path. The deft balancing of *yin* and *yang* is needed to resolve contradictions; otherwise, opposing forces might tear an organization apart. Jack Ma of Alibaba is reputed to travel to work with the Daoist text *Dao De Jing* in his briefcase, and preach the wisdom of Daoist thought when managing his staff.

Daoist influence is also felt indirectly in Japan where Buddhism had been steadily imbibed in the past. Its leavening influence has evolved into Zen which, together with Shinto, pervade the psyche of the Japanese and subtly influence their governance culture.

In Japan, Confucianism and Buddhism exist side by side with indigenous Shinto and the samurai legacy to produce a potent mix that characterized the dynamic Tokugawa era (Chapter 5). This was followed by Japan's rise as an imperialistic power with the Meiji Restoration. The Meiji era also produced some of the most powerful corporations in the world run on the entity model. However, in contemporary times, this also led to a collision with the shareholder wealth-maximizing objectives of foreign investors. The recent sagas of Japanese corporate icons Toyota, Olympus, Toshiba, and Nissan in many ways reflect this clash of cultures. In our studies of these cases, as well as of the iconic Ina Corporation, we see how traditional values have resisted the onslaught of the foreign shareholders' wealth-maximizing creed.

In South Korea, the rise of *chaebols* after World War II eventually saw these huge state-sponsored conglomerates lapse into the abuse of authoritarian power by their corporate patriarchs (Chapter 6). Despite decades of attempts by the government to rein them in to meet minimal governance standards of international corporations, companies like Samsung remain firmly in the grip of family members steeped in Confucian top-down management.

Singapore presents a unique and fascinating case of a city-state run like a large corporation by a political party that makes no apologies for its soft authoritarian governance (Chapter 7). The ruling party has been returned with overwhelming majorities for over half a century, achieving the feat with a strong benevolent leadership that adeptly harnesses liberal democratic institutions to consolidate its power. But power without sufficient checks and balances can lead to lapses. Add the electoral weight of Millennials who place higher emphasis on personal freedoms and the adequacy of checks and balances, and there may be a case for a paradigm shift in the governance model.

Do cultural values determine success in economic growth? This question has been vigorously debated in the context of East Asian values (Chapter 8). Drawing on the logic of causation from the philosophy of science, I argue that this question is a spurious one. Economic success, like events in history, can never be attributed to a single principal cause, and attempts to over-simplify it to a dominant causal factor usually only reflect the biases and vested interests of the perpetrators of such explanations.

Meritocratic democracy

Although Edmund Burke's dictum that a system of government should be consonant with the country's culture appears reasonable, if not self-evident, it is surprising how many leaders in the West still try to foist their value systems on other civilizations (Chapter 9). As a result, a distinction has emerged, mostly in the Western media, between a democracy and an authoritarian state. This is a false dichotomy.

It would appear that the West has appropriated the term "democracy" to mean "Western liberal democracy" in which universal suffrage, free elections, and the mandate to rule is handed to the politically popular. In reality, various shades of democracy exist, from liberal to authoritarian. For most of the non-Western world, there is a broader usage of the term, in line with the Oxford Dictionary's definition: "A form of government in which the people have a voice in the exercise of power, typically through elected representatives."[2] A democracy by this definition would include soft authoritarian democracies like Singapore. A hard single-party regime would have a weaker claim, although political thinkers in China do assert that the country has her own unique brand of democracy. Indeed, the new constitution contemplated by scholars like Jiang Qing and Yu Keping proposes a revised political system rooted in Confucian benevolence and keeping the concentration of power in a ruling group. Such a constitution, however, would still have to demonstrate the presence of safeguards against abuses of human rights.

It would be helpful to strip authoritarianism of its pejorative connotations so as to distinguish it from tyranny and dictatorship. Authoritarianism can be used in a neutral sense to denote a style of governance in which the benefit of effective leadership through the exercise of authority comes at the cost of reductions in (not the absence of) personal freedoms.[3] Students of business management are familiar with the authoritarian inclination of corporate leadership. Chief executives and boards of directors do not routinely seek the approval of the company's employees when setting out major policies and strategies for the company, although they would be wise to consult them. Authoritarianism, as practised in state governance by some regimes, has been harsh on human rights, but in places like Singapore and Taiwan (in her earlier phase of development), it has been relatively benign and notably successful. Thus, it is important for authoritarian governance *not* to have a cruel edge, and for the people in such regimes to realize that there are orderly means to remove a bad leader.

I have proposed the term "meritocratic democracy" for state governance in which leaders are chosen by proven ability in management, rather than popularity with the masses. In practice, depending on their historical and cultural legacies, meritocratic democracies come in different shades. In East Asia, they tend to be more authoritarian than liberal democracies in the West. Liberal democracies in recent years appear to have become increasingly dysfunctional.[4] Perhaps some variant of meritocratic democracy would be a useful reference model for reforming systems of government in other parts of the world. Liberal democracy has produced many good governments, as well as some very bad ones. Authoritarian regimes have caused untold misery when a "bad emperor" gets into power, but a few have produced sterling results. It behooves each nation to find a system of governance that is compatible with its cultural and historical legacy.

Disclaimer

This book does not present primary research findings on culture and governance in East Asia. Rather, it leverages the rich literature on the subject as well as my experience as a corporate chief executive, business school professor and dean, and a Member of the Singapore Parliament. More significantly, it reflects the deep interest in culture that led me, years after completing graduate work in economics, to study and research philosophy, Chinese literature, and East Asian history. I am sure there are lapses in academic rigour in my down-to-earth arguments but take comfort that the general reader interested in the big picture will be more forgiving.

Most of all, I urge the reader to cast aside stereotypes about how democratic governance and corporate governance should be practised. Instead, start from first principles that are distilled from a deeper understanding of history and culture.

Notes

1 *Datsu-A Ron* was an anonymously written editorial published in *Jiji Shimpo* on 16 March 1885. The title "Datsu-A Ron" has been translated in a number of ways, including "Leaving Asia," "Shedding Asia," "Goodbye Asia," and "Discarding Asia." Although the piece was originally published anonymously, it has been attributed to writer and educator Fukuzawa Yukichi on account that it appears in Volume 10 of his complete works. See Fukuzawa Yukichi (1960) [1885]), pp. 238–40, quoted in Pekka Korhonen (2019), p. 3 and Torsten Weber (2017), p. 66.
2 Stevenson and Waite (2011), p. 381.
3 This usage of "authoritarianism" is in line with Stevenson and Waite (2011), p. 88.
4 See, for example, Deneen (2018).

References

Patrick J. Deneen. (2018). *Why Liberalism Failed*. New Haven, CT: Yale University Press.
Fukuzawa Yukichi. (1960). *Fukuzawa Yukichi zenshu, dai 10 kan*. Tokyo: Iwanami shoten. (*Original work published in 1885*).

Pekka Korhonen. (2019). *"Leaving Asia? The Meaning of Datsu-A and Japan's Modern History."* *The Asia-Pacific Journal* 11 (50–1): 1–19. Available online at https://apjjf.org/2014/11/50/Pekka-Korhonen/4083/article.html. Accessed 16 July 2019.

Angus Stevenson and Maurice Waite (eds.). (2011). "Democracy and Authoritarian." In *Concise Oxford English Dictionary*, 12th edition. Oxford: Oxford University Press.

Torsten Weber. (2017). *Embracing 'Asia' in China and Japan: Asianism Discourse and the Contest for Hegemony, 1912–1933.* Cham, Switzerland: Palgrave Macmillan.

1

FROM *HUANGDI* TO XI JINPING

A brief cultural history of China

When Voltaire declared that the organization of the Chinese empire was "in truth the best that the world has ever seen," the merits of Chinese governance were little known in the West. Even in the early twentieth century, German intellectuals were only starting to appreciate the sophistication of Chinese civilization; the philosopher Hermann von Keyserling considered China "the highest universal culture of being hitherto known."[1]

Although the Summer Palace was admired by some European intellectuals, rampaging British and French troops had little idea of the sacrilege they were committing when they burned it down in 1890. They destroyed most of the priceless art treasures from three millennia, and stole much of the rest to sell for puny gains. As a senseless act, it was worse than the destruction of ancient Roman ruins in Palmyra by the Islamic State militants in 2017, which drew international condemnation.[2]

China had been one of the richest and most enduring cultures in human history for three millennia. The hundred years of humiliation she endured from the start of the Opium Wars in 1839–1860 was a bitter pill to swallow. Throughout those dark days of Western imperialist oppression, the Chinese never lost confidence in the superiority of their culture. They continued to refer to Western invaders as "barbarians." In so doing, they placed these Westerners invaders in the same category as Mongol horsemen from the north who had conquered China only to be overthrown by mandarins armed with centuries-old wisdom.

In this chapter, we will take the reader through a selective review of highlights of Chinese cultural history, so as to provide the necessary background for assessing how culture continues to influence governance and management in contemporary China and East Asia.

China in antiquity

Chinese history is usually thought to have begun five thousand years ago with the legendary "Three Sovereigns and Five Emperors" (*sanhuang wudi* 三皇五帝). Of these, emperors Yao and Shun have been revered as wise and benevolent rulers. The emperor *Huangdi* or the "Yellow Emperor"[3] is credited with developing medical practices to improve health, longevity, and harmony with nature. These practices were compiled two millennia later in the classic *The Yellow Emperor's Canon of Medicine* (*Huangdi Neijing* 黄帝内经).

The first dynasty, the Xia (夏) (circa 2100–1600 BC), is regarded as largely mythological, as there are few reliable written records of the period. However, archaeological findings show the existence of an agrarian civilization centred in northern China around present-day Shanxi, Shaanxi, and Henan provinces.

The Xia was followed by the Shang Dynasty (商) (circa 1600–1122 BC). Under the Shang, complex urban settlements and social stratification emerged. Bronze castings and oracle inscriptions on tortoise shells (sometimes called oracle bone inscriptions in English) represent some of the earliest Chinese art and literary forms. Because words were laboriously carved on tortoise shells (*jia gu wen*), economy of expression was needed. Hence, written texts were terse and concise. Extensive use was made of anecdotes and narratives to convey complex ideas in a few words. This is not unlike the Western idiomatic use of shorthand devices such as "Trojan horse," meaning a ruse used to gain entry into enemy ground. Because of the difficulty in producing such concise language, only those who had studied history and the classics could read and write with confidence. Literacy became the preserve of an elite few, which ensured a high degree of social stratification up until the May Fourth Movement of 1919 when plain language (*baihua*) was adopted. This simplification put reading and writing within reach of the masses.

The resultant explosion in literacy had far-reaching social implications. It allowed the common people to read political literature and posters, and gave them access to the wisdom of the ancients through classics written in spoken language. In the late twentieth century, mass literacy played a crucial role in the country's economic development.

Zhou dynasty

The Zhou dynasty (周) (1122–221 BC), which lasted for over nine hundred years, was a period of significant cultural progress. It saw the rise of philosophical thought, the emergence of a state bureaucracy, and the study of military strategies as the art of war.

The "Hundred Schools of Thought" phenomenon that flourished from the sixth century BC to 221 BC was an era during which there was vigorous contention among scholars.[4] Owing to the immense cultural and intellectual energy of this period, an unusually broad range of ideas was freely debated, some of which would influence societies in East Asia. The most influential of these schools of thought were Confucianism, Daoism, Legalism, and Mohism. Of these, Confucianism and Daoism would eventually expand and gain dominance in Chinese society up to modern times.

The Legalists saw human nature as inherently selfish. They advocated that the only means of preserving social order was strict discipline and the enforcement of law, with severe punishments for the recalcitrant. It exalted the state as coming before all else, and maintained social order by empowering the state through wealth and military strength. Legalist philosophy retains some influence among a number of present-day East Asian authoritarian regimes.

Proponents of Mohism, named after founding father Mozi (470–391 BC), saw everyone as equal under heaven and preached universal love. The Mohists disapproved of partiality towards one's own family members, and wanted officials to be appointed on the basis of ability and compassion for common folk. It was a gentle philosophy that did not survive the tyrannical Qin emperor who ended the Zhou dynasty.

It was the pragmatic social ethics of Confucian thought and the wisdom of Daoist harmony with nature that survived despotic rulers and dynastic upheavals. The teachings of Confucius (Figure 1.1) and his disciple Mencius, and the thoughts of Daoism founder Laozi (Figure 1.2) and disciple Zhuangzi, have remained the staple of students of Chinese philosophy. They continue to be enduring influences over the spiritual consciousness of Chinese civilization and underlie its resilience.

FIGURE 1.1 Confucius, the teacher and moral philosopher[5]

FIGURE 1.2 Laozi, gentle founder of Daoism[6]

Sunzi and the Art of War and the brilliant strategies of the later Zhou period (known as the Warring States) were distillations of the musings of fertile minds that considered all political and military situations to determine where strategic genius could be applied to gain victory. A thousand years later, these strategies were edited and rewritten as the classic manual on intrigue, *The Thirty-Six Strategies* (sometimes translated into English as *The Thirty-Six Stratagems*).

United under one emperor

The chaos of the Warring States period ended when the first emperor defeated rival states and unified them under the Qin dynasty. It was a creative if short and violent dynasty. The Qin emperor established standards of measure and currency for exchange, and started building the Great Wall to keep out northern barbarians.

Attempts to attain immortality finally resulted in his death, when he was poisoned by one of the elixirs of life he imbibed. The dynasty collapsed during the reign of an incompetent son who was weighed down by a creaky, hapless administrative structure unfit for a vast nation. *Qinshi Huangdi*, the first emperor of a united China, left behind an immense mausoleum with thousands of terracotta soldiers guarding his final resting place.

A principal reason for the quick fall of Qin was the first emperor's rejection of Confucian thought. Confucian scholars had exhorted him to show benevolence to his subjects and observe the rules of propriety laid down by the great sage. In response to their earnest representations in court, *Qinshi Huangdi* buried them alive and burned all the Confucian texts he could find.

Without the scholars and their administrative skills, the dynasty crumbled, making way for one of the greatest Chinese dynasties.

From Han to Ming

The Han dynasty (汉) (202 BC–AD 220) saw the development of a formal structure of civil service, a central government, and provincial governments. Education in the ancient classics flourished. The invention of paper allowed careful records to be made of administrative decisions and enabled the propagation of government experience to the far reaches of the empire. Advances in farming during this period ensured that even though droughts and pestilence continued to plague Chinese life, starvation was reduced to periods of bad harvests.

The medical classic *Huangdi Neijing*, compiled during this period, rejected the ancient mythology of spirits and demons as causes of disease. Drawing on Daoist holistic philosophy, illness was attributed to natural climatic forces, human emotions, and poor lifestyles. Healing methods were developed according to the physicians' clinical experience. The *Neijing* is the authoritative text on the tenets of Chinese medicine even today. Its emphasis on diet and living habits for the prevention of disease continues to be the basis of Chinese health cultivation. Its insight into internal imbalances of the body as the basic cause of illness stands in contrast to the importance of aetiology in Western medicine, which emphasizes microorganisms and cellular malfunction.

The concept of balance and harmony within the body, where *yin* and *yang* check and balance each other, has deep implications for the management of social order. It is the basis for attaining social harmony through the management of opposing forces in society to restrain and complement rather than destroy each other. As we shall see later (in Chapter 4, "Daoism and Management"), this aspect of Chinese thought represents the essence of Chinese wisdom. It eschews absolutes like the primacy of personal freedom and the stubborn insistence that only one form of governance is correct for all worlds.

At the end of the Han dynasty, a strong prime minister and a weak young emperor set the scene for the fall of the dynasty. Cao Cao was a political genius, brilliant military strategist, and accomplished poet. As prime minister, he usurped the power of the emperor without seizing the throne, a move that would have been unacceptable in Han Confucian culture.

The country then split into three kingdoms – Shu, led by Liu Bei, uncle of the young emperor; Wu, led by Sun Quan in the south; and Wei in the north controlled by Cao Cao. The forty-five-year struggle among them to gain control of the country bore witness to daring military exploits and ingenious political intrigue. This tumultuous period was later immortalized in the Ming novel *The Romance of the Three Kingdoms*.

Cao Cao eventually triumphed but respected Confucian loyalty to the sovereign by not usurping the throne. It was left to his son to establish the Wei dynasty, which marked the beginning of a long miserable period of Chinese history.

Wei-Jin and North-South dynasties (魏晋南北朝) (220–581)

Sometimes regarded as the Dark Ages of China, the Wei-Jin and North and South dynasties did not comprise one continuous dynasty but a series of short-lived dynasties, some coterminous with others. The country was fragmented, with some regions uniting briefly, only to be torn asunder again.

Life was harsh under the string of despotic rulers and warlords of this period. Unlike life during the Dark Ages in Europe, art and poetry continued to flourish, and philosophy took a turn towards the spiritual. Common folk raised on a staple of Confucian rigours found solace in the philosophy of Daoism. Renouncing fame and fortune by going with the flow of nature and living a wandering life in the vales and mountains was, for many, a comforting alternative to the discipline of Confucianism ethics.

This trying period ended some 360 years later with the reunification of the nation under the brief reign of the Sui emperors (581–605). The stage was thus set for the splendour of the Tang and Song dynasties in the next six hundred years.

Tang and Song dynasties

The Tang dynasty (唐) (618–907) was a socially liberal period when women dressed lavishly and imperial concubines enjoyed political influence. The dynasty also boasted the only female emperor in Chinese history, Wu Zetian.

Tang poetry, arguably the greatest achievement of Chinese literature, flourished with luminaries like Li Bai, Du Fu, and Wang Wei. Li Bai, the romantic who inclined towards the mystical, was the closest of the three to Daoism. Du Fu was the quintessential Confucian patriot, as he wrote with deep feeling about the horrors of war and the suffering of the poor. Wang Wei, a senior court official, was a Buddhist with Daoist inclinations.

Chinese culture spread to neighbouring countries, particularly Japan, who imported Chinese written characters to form the first building blocks of her own syllabary. Buddhism also crossed the seas and evolved into Zen Buddhism in the ninth century, when monks studying Zen in China returned to Japan to preach the religion.

During the Song dynasty (宋) (960–1226), China was the world leader in technology, manufacturing, and political thought and governance. Education expanded rapidly with the introduction of printed books. The dynasty saw the rise of the land-owning scholar-gentry ruling class. Passing the civil service examinations opened the way to not only to officialdom, but also to wealth.

A new form of poetry broke free from the formal structure of Tang verse, subsequently becoming a form of singing enjoyed by common folk. Among the great Song poets was Su Dongpo, a renaissance man who not only held official posts, but also mastered Chinese medicine and culinary skills. He invented the savoury *Dongpo rou* pork dish bearing his name. This dish remains much loved in Chinese cuisine today.

The prominent Song dynasty Neo-Confucianist Zhu Xi drew inspiration from Buddhist thought as well as Daoist philosophy, synthesizing concepts from the *Book of Changes*, such as growth and flourishing, with Confucian humaneness and ritual.[7]

The Song dynasty ended with the Mongolian invasion. The Mongols were horse-riding warriors who never learnt to use Confucian principles in state administration. These sword-wielding marauders from the northern steppes found ruling a vast land with a civilization far more advanced and sophisticated than theirs too much of a challenge, and the Mongol or *Yuan* dynasty ended in less than a century.

The Ming dynasty that followed saw Chinese ceramics reach a new level of refinement. Daoism and Buddhism, which had by now taken root deeply in the Chinese psyche, inevitably permeated Confucianism. Neo-Confucianism that flourished in the Song period reached a high point under the Ming emperors, as scholars delved deeper into its spiritual aspect in their search for an ethical life.

As with all dynasties, decay gradually crept in, laying the groundwork for yet another invasion from the north.

The Qing dynasty (清) (1644–1912) and the founding of the Republic

The last Chinese dynasty started well, with capable emperors like Kangxi and Qianlong, who had learnt from the mistakes of the Mongols. They studied the classics and ensured that their successors were as knowledgeable in Chinese culture as the Chinese officials appointed to serve them.

Towards the end of the dynasty, China came into violent encounter with the military power of "red-haired barbarians" (i.e., the white Westerners) who had sailed in from the South China Sea. The Opium Wars saw the Qing army routed by the English, marking the beginning of a hundred years of humiliation and soul-searching by the mandarins. Was the Chinese civilization with its exquisite art, rich literature, Confucian ethics, and Daoist wisdom helpless against mere "barbarian" firepower?

The answer came in the May Fourth Movement of 1919 when over 4,000 students from Peking, Yenching, and other universities gathered in Tiananmen and marched in protest against the Treaty of Versailles, which had ceded former German concessions in the Shandong peninsula to Japan. In reality, it was a pragmatic reaction to aggression because the adoption of Western science and technology and some of its political ideas enabled China to strengthen its ability to resist imperialism. The May Fourth Movement marked the beginning of Chinese modernization, providing the country with the economic and military capacity to resist foreign aggression.[8] To beat the West at their own game, they needed to upgrade their understanding of science and technology, and combine that with the ancient strategies from *Sunzi and the Art of War* and *The Thirty-Six Strategies*.

With fall of the Qing dynasty in 1911, a period of instability followed. Sun Yat-sen, who led the revolution to topple the Qing dynasty, proved inept at peacetime leadership. Warlords contended with each other for power. The Japanese invasion of Manchuria turned into a protracted war that ended only with the defeat of Japan in 1945.

In the civil war that ensued, the Americans backed the losing side led by Generalissimo Chiang Kai-shek, whose wealthy Wellesley College–educated wife Soong Mei-ling charmed the US Congress with promises of building a liberal democratic China in the image of America.

An autodidact, Mao Zedong, who read widely in the Peking University library where he worked, emerged victorious after rallying the masses to his cause. During the epic Long March, some 100,000 soldiers covered 9,000 kilometres on foot over punishing terrain from Guanxi in the southwest to the Ya'an caves in the north. Accounts of their bravery and revolutionary zeal inspired an entire literary genre.

Mao's disciplined troops refrained from plundering farms and villages en route to Ya'an. Instead, they showed Confucian benevolence, gratefully receiving food and supplies from peasants, and even recruiting many into Mao's army. Their victory was foreseen by writer Edgar Snow,[9] who lived among them and witnessed firsthand their fervour and commitment, which told a different story from the dispatches of American agents stationed in China.

After the 1949 Chinese Communist Revolution, Mao adopted Marxist economic and social philosophy, which was alien to traditional Chinese culture. Confucian values were rejected during the disastrous Cultural Revolution (1966–1976) when children ignored filial piety and reported their parents for crimes of capitalism against the state.

Deng Xiaoping emerged from the chaos to introduce market reforms "with Chinese characteristics," thus radically transforming the economy. But the desire to get rich eroded traditional values and undermined society's moral foundations.

This led current President Xi Jinping to announce in 2014 that Confucian virtue would be fostered once more in the country, as Confucian teaching would be reinstituted in schools.

Summary of Chinese historical periods

Legendary period

From around 3000 BC – Legendary Emperors (The Yellow Emperor, Yao, Shun, etc.)
Xia Dynasty 夏 (approximately 2100–1600 BC)

Ancient China: recorded history beginning with the Shang Dynasty

Shang Dynasty 商 (approximately 1600–1122 BC)
Zhou Dynasty 周 (1122–221 BC)

Western Zhou (1122–771 BC)
Eastern Zhou (771–256 BC)

(a) Spring and Autumn Period 春秋 (772–481 BC)
(b) The Warring States Period 战国 (403–221 BC)

United under the Qin emperor

Qin Dynasty 秦, under Qin Shi Huang Di, also known as the First Emperor of China (221–207 BC)
Han Dynasty 汉 (202 BC–AD 220)
Three Kingdoms Period 三国 (AD 220–265); China was fragmented during this period
Wei-Jin, North-South Dynasties 魏晋南北朝 (AD 220–589)

Golden age of Chinese poetry

Sui Dynasty 隋 (581–618)
Tang Dynasty 唐 (618–907)
Five Dynasties (907–960); China was fragmented during this period
Song Dynasty 宋 (960–1226), divided into Northern Song and Southern Song

Invasions from the North

Yuan Dynasty 元, also known as the Mongol Dynasty (1279–1368)
Ming Dynasty 明 (1368–1644)
Qing Dynasty 清, also known as the Manchu Dynasty (1644–1912)

Modern China

1912, The Chinese Revolution (辛亥革命), led by Sun Yat-sen
1919, May Fourth Movement (五四运动)
1937–1945, Sino-Japanese War (抗日时期)
1945–1949, Chinese Civil War between the Kuomintang (KMT) and the Chinese Communist Party
1949, Liberation (解放)
1966–1976, The Cultural Revolution (文化大革命)
1978, Economic Revolution under Deng Xiaoping
2014, Xi Jinping revives Confucianism

Notes

1 Durant (1935), p. 639.
2 Bilefsky (2017).
3 This popular but misguided translation of *Huangdi* (the Huang emperor) derives from the surname "Huang," which is also the Chinese word for the colour yellow. Calling him "the Yellow Emperor" is as corny as calling Gordon Brown, former prime minister of the United Kingdom, "the Brown Prime Minister."

4 Loewe and Shaughnessy (1999), p. 16.
5 From Konfuzius-1770.jpg – Wikimedia https://commons.wikimedia.org/wiki/File:
   Konfuzius-1770.jpg.
6 From Laozi_Daodejing – Wikimedia https://commons.wikimedia.org/wiki/File:Laozi_
   Daodejing.jpg.
7 Thompson (2017).
8 Schwarcz (1986), pp. 283–302. Some Western scholars have followed Schwarcz (1986),
   and called the May Fourth Movement "the Chinese Enlightenment," comparing it to the
   eighteenth-century transition of Europe. This is because the enlightenment in Europe saw
   a shift away from intellectual domination by the church to rational philosophies, whereby
   faith in the laws of the universe was explored through the Scientific Revolution.
9 See Edgar Snow (1937).

References

Dan Bilefsky. (2017). "ISIS Destroys Part of Roman Theater in Palmyra, Syria." *The New York
   Times*, 20 January. Available online at www.nytimes.com/2017/01/20/world/middleeast/
   palmyra-syria-isis-amphitheater.html. Accessed 16 July 2019.
Will Durant. (1935). *Our Oriental Heritage.* New York: Simon and Schuster.
Michael Loewe and Edward L. Shaughnessy. (1999). *The Cambridge History of Ancient China:
   From the Origins of Civilization to 221 BC.* Cambridge and New York: Cambridge Uni-
   versity Press.
Vera Schwarcz. (1986). *The Chinese Enlightenment: Intellectuals and the Legacy of the May Fourth
   Movement of 1919.* Berkeley and Los Angeles, CA: University of California Press.
Edgar Snow. (1937). *Red Star over China.* New York: Random House.
Kirill Thompson. (2017). "Zhu Xi." In Edward N. Zalta (ed.), *Stanford Encyclopedia of Phi-
   losophy.* Stanford, CA: Stanford University. (First published on 3 September 2015). Available online at https://plato.stanford.edu/archives/sum2017/entries/zhu-xi/. Accessed
   12 April 2019.

2

CONFUCIAN VALUES AND PEOPLE MANAGEMENT

A country of a thousand war chariots cannot be administered unless the ruler shows affection towards his subjects.

(The Analects of Confucius)

In 2008, one of the most troubling scandals in Chinese corporate history unfolded to a stunned global audience. Best-selling Chinese brand Sanlu – China's largest diary producer and the second largest in the world – had poisoned 290,000 infants with milk powder tainted with melamine. Melamine, a chemical used in plastic manufacturing, had been used to increase the protein content of the milk, which could then be diluted whilst carrying the same protein content. 51,900 babies were hospitalized and 11 died. It was organized crime for cost-cutting and profit, involving top management and suspected conniving regulators.[1]

What caused one of China's leading and most respected firms to endanger the lives of millions of infants in a culture that treasures the nurturing of children? How did raw greed drive men and women – most of whom were themselves parents – to risk innocent lives on a massive scale? Whatever happened to the vaunted traditional Confucian values of benevolence and righteousness?

Investigations revealed that tainting milk for profit was a widespread practice, and that a conspiracy of silence had pervaded the industry, possibly involving regulatory watchdogs as well. An international observer described the incident as the manifestation of "capitalism without ethics," a cesspool into which Chinese corporate culture had sunk by the beginning of the twenty-first century. This was only thirty years after Deng Xiaoping's economic revolution of 1978 had unleashed unbridled greed in a nation that had produced, arguably, the greatest moralist in human history.[2]

There have been many more disturbing accounts of the degradation of enterprise culture in the new China, such as rice made from plastic, expensive tonic cordyceps with poisonous lead filaments implanted to increase their weight, and cooking oil scooped up from sewers for use in restaurants. Has the birthplace of Confucius, whose ethical philosophy influenced China and its East Asian neighbours for over two thousand years, lost its moral fibre in the frenzied scramble for wealth?

The unhappy truth is that by the beginning of the twenty-first century, the pursuit of wealth had blinded many Chinese to their traditional moral compass. The morally weak society that troubled the sage Confucius in the Spring-Autumn period of the Zhou dynasty seemed to have re-emerged in contemporary China, presenting a new challenge to the leadership of the country. The Sanlu scandal was only one of many that were waiting to happen. It was symptomatic of a retreat from traditional Confucian values.

Rise and fall of Confucianism

Although Confucianism as a moral philosophy was founded by the sage Confucius, or Kong Fuzi as he is known in Chinese (孔夫子) (551–479 BC), in the intellectually vibrant Spring and Autumn period, many of its precepts had long been practised earlier in Chinese culture. Decorum, kindness and filial piety were part and parcel of Chinese upbringing. But the harsh realities of surviving in a tumultuous society brought out man's darker impulses. China in the times of Confucius was a cultured society with a ruling mandarin class that was steeped in poetry, art, and spiritual cultivation. Unfortunately, most of the mandarins were also often obsessed with the pursuit of wealth and power. Emperors were despotic, and subjects survived by cunning and deceit. It was in this socially toxic environment that a despairing young man decided he could no longer allow humanity to further degenerate. While he acknowledged that human nature could not be changed, he firmly believed it must be moulded for the sake of a harmonious society.

As recorded in the dialogues in *The Analects*,[3] Confucius devoted much of his time to princes and kings, urging them to show benevolence to their subjects so as to gain their respect and loyalty. Confucianism was almost obliterated after the Zhou dynasty, when the Qin Emperor burned Confucian texts and buried Confucian scholars alive. By the time of the Han dynasty, Confucian ethics underwent a strong revival, and became entrenched as the state ideology. Princes in the imperial courts spent much of their growing years studying Confucian classics. They were provided with the best tutors in the land. Each tutor would nurse the hope that his protégé would one day ascend to the throne. For the next two thousand years, Confucianism became embedded in Chinese culture as the foundation of ethics and social conduct for rulers, merchants, soldiers, and peasants alike.

It was not until foreign Marxist ideology sprouted in Chinese soil in the first half of the twentieth century that Confucianism faced its greatest existential crisis since the rule of the Qin emperor. Following Mao's rise to power in the Chinese Communist Revolution of 1949, brutal political campaigns attacked the so-called four olds, namely old customs, practices, living habits, and ideas. The failed economic reforms of Mao's Great Leap Forward impelled a close comrade and veteran of the Long March, Peng Dehuai, to challenge his supreme authority. This precipitated the historic 1959 Lushan Conference which ended in the political purge of Peng. To consolidate his power and prestige among the masses, Mao launched the disastrous Cultural Revolution of 1966–1976. Millions of youths were set loose with little red books of Mao aphorisms. The result was desecration of the ancient values of filial piety and respect for elders. Children reported on their ideologically "decadent" parents, elders, and teachers. Leading intellectuals and literary luminaries were driven to suicide for having stood by traditional values.[4]

Confucian values were further eroded following the 3rd Plenary Session of the 11th Central Committee of the Communist Party of China in 1978. In a historic change of course, Deng Xiaoping advocated economic pragmatism as the solution to China's flagging economic development. The new ideology was captured by his famous quip that it did not matter if a cat was black or white as long as it could catch mice. In a daring repudiation of Marxist egalitarianism, Deng extolled the pursuit to wealth, famously declaring, "To be rich is glorious." It unleashed not only Keynesian "animal spirits," but also a torrent of pent-up greed.

The result was the greatest economic drama in human history. Over a billion Chinese were catapulted from the poverty trap of a backward country plagued by famine and deprivation, and transformed into a confident people that could boast of being behind the world's largest online spending in a single day in 2018. China's rise has been so rapid that it has elicited push-back from the American far right and raised the spectre of a Thucydides's Trap war between the two superpowers.[5]

The decline in traditional values, worship of money, and vain consumerism brought predictable consequences. Corruption and commercial scams proliferated. With the power of patronage of government officials, the attainment of power conferred by officialdom became the corollary object of the chase. As the Chinese folk saying goes, *you quan jiu you qian* (有权就有钱), meaning "With power comes wealth." Two generations, i.e., the youths of the Cultural Revolution and their children, grew up with little or no moral compass. Women from respectable families, including housewives, sold their bodies, leading to the saying *xiao pin bu xiao chang* (笑贫不笑娼), meaning "Deride the poor, but not the whore." Similarly, men risked imprisonment, and even death, to get rich quickly.

Reviving Confucianism as state ideology

Against this backdrop of declining moral values, the government introduced the study of the classic *Guoxue* (国学), and President Xi Jinping made a high-profile announcement of the revival of Confucian teachings in 2014. There was clearly also a political dimension to this about-face. By reinstating a state ideology that promoted traditional culture and mores, the government was also emphasizing China's historical legacy of governance where power was concentrated in the hands of a ruling elite. Describing the classics as the "genes" of Chinese culture, Xi declared:

"Confucianism, along with other philosophies and cultures taking shape and grow-ing within China, are records of spiritual experiences, rational thinking and cultural achievements of the nation during its striving to build its home. These cultures have nourished the flourishing Chinese nation."[6] Xi stated further that the Chinese Com-munist Party is "the successor to and promoter of fine traditional Chinese culture."[7]

The campaign to foster Confucian values drew international attention with many commentators making much of the obvious, that Xi's intentions were politi-cal rather than ethical.[8] Detractors argued that Confucianism was out of step with modernity because Confucian feudal hierarchy had been replaced by social equality and propriety (rites) by rule of law. However, Zhang Yiwu of Peking University was quick to point out that Confucianism and traditional values were still relevant because Chinese society remains more governed by social relations than by laws.[9]

Martin Jacques emphasizes China as a "civilizational-state" with Confucianism as her secular ideology.[10] Sébastien Billioud contends that the revived interest in classical texts reflects "a spiritual dimension of self-cultivation" inherent in Confu-cian rituals in public ceremonies (Figure 2.1); this in turn inspires intellectuals to call for the reinstatement of Confucianism as a state or civil religion.[11]

The need to articulate a state ideology has gained fresh urgency in light of an emerging multipolar world order in which *power diffusion*, in Joseph Nye's language, sees power transition from the lone superpower America to a number of states. China stands out among these states, offering a rational alternative to the American gospel of unfettered individual freedom and human rights.[12]

FIGURE 2.1 Confucian activists honouring Mencius in Zoucheng, Shandong province

Source: © 2011 / Sébastien Billioud[13]

Confucianism and people management

From the point of view of corporate and state management, Confucian ethics has profound implications for people management, as will be obvious when we consider some of its core precepts. In some ways, Confucius could claim to be the first pragmatic thinker in the art of human resource management.

The teachings of Confucius were compiled by his students in one volume, *Lun Yu* (论语) or *The Analects*. *The Analects* and other writings that followed are rich examples of the dialectical debates between the sage and various kings and rulers. Confucius's most prominent follower was Mengzi or Mencius (372–289 BC), who hailed from Eastern Zhou during the Warring States period. Mencius was bold and incisive in his writings and discourse with fellow philosophers. He advocated removing a ruler, by force if necessary, should the ruler be found to be unjust and could not be prevailed upon to change his ways. Mencius believed that people are inherently good, and that education and society ought to bring out this inherent goodness. This was in contrast to another Confucian thinker Xunzi, who believed in the inherent evil and selfishness of man, likening man to animals in the wild because man cared only for himself. This viewpoint was later taken up by Han Feizi of the Legalistic school, who believed that law and punishment were the only effective means of keeping man's evil nature in check.

Although Confucius had faith in the inherent goodness of man, and in the ability of kindness and love to reform a wayward person, he knew that mankind would not always let better instincts prevail in society. It was therefore necessary to inculcate a code of moral conduct to bring out his good nature.

The Analects and the eponymous *Mencius* have remained the principal references for Confucian philosophy. These are the core Confucian precepts that have had held enduring sway over China and many parts of East Asia:

1   Ren (仁):[14] humanity, benevolence, and an affective concern for the well-being of others
2   Li (礼): rites, protocol and decorum are the traditional norms governing conduct between people according to their social positions
3   Yi (义): justice and righteousness
4   Zhong (忠): loyalty to one's ruler, parents and friends
5   Xiao (孝): filial piety

Confucius was a moral and political philosopher ahead of his time because he proffered a way out of the conflict and strife in states ruled by despots and greedy ministers. He sought to achieve this without appealing to a higher spiritual authority like God or to the existence of natural virtues found in the metaphysics of Plato's forms.[15]

As a pragmatist, he insisted that man be nurtured in proper behaviour, with respect for the authority and the wisdom of family elders and rulers. Respect for authority would be ingrained from a young age by observance of the proper protocols or rites (*li*). In turn, elders and rulers show benevolence (*ren*) to win trust and support. The twin values of *ren* and *li* thus form the essence of human management.

Ren *in human resource management*

Commonly translated as benevolence, *ren* defies simple definition. To say that it is an affective concern for fellow men is ambiguous, as it understates its centrality in Chinese morality. To regard it as humanity in the loftiest sense of the term is to make it a universal and impartial kind of love for humankind, regardless of clan, race, or creed. This was implied in the Confucian classic, *The Doctrine of the Mean* (中庸), which advocates "Benevolence is humanity" (人者仁也); and in *The Book of Rites* (礼记.礼运) that states "The world is one community" (天下为公).[16] Yet in practice, as has been observed by Fei Xiaotong, Chinese society consists of relationship networks where not everyone gets equal treatment. Family and clan members closest to each person are the objects of the highest level of benevolence, while unknown people in distant lands receive the least.[17] The utilitarian nature of benevolence is highlighted in a line from *Analects* 1.5:

> A country of a thousand war chariots cannot be administered unless the ruler . . . shows affection towards his subjects in general and uses the labour of the peasantry only at the proper times of year.[18]

A big country cannot be administered well if the leader does not have affection and concern for his subjects and compels them to work hard in harsh winters or in searing summer heat. The king's subjects, treated with benevolence, willingly toil for him and are easier to govern. By emphasizing the practical benefits of showing benevolence, Confucius was the human resource manager *par excellence*. Indeed, much of modern Western management of human resources is built around winning employee loyalty through looking after their welfare.

In the modern corporation, *ren* expressed towards society at large translates into corporate social responsibility. By discharging its moral obligation to society and the environments in which they operate, the corporation wins social recognition and approbation, which are good for profitability in the long run.

Viewed in this light, *ren* is conditional and instrumental. It does not have the purity and universality of unconditional Christian love ("charity") as expressed in I Corinthians 13 of the Holy Bible (King James version):

> Though I speak with the tongues of men and of angels, and have not charity, I am become as sounding brass, or a tinkling cymbal. And though I have the gift of prophecy, and understand all mysteries, and all knowledge; and though I have all faith, so that I could remove mountains, and have not charity, I am nothing. And though I bestow all my goods to feed the poor, and though I give my body to be burned, and have not charity, it profiteth me nothing.

In the ideal of Christian love, one can give up all of one's possessions and even one's life, but they amount to nothing if motivated by anything but pure love. Dostoyevsky captures a similar notion through the concept of "real love" in a memorable passage from *The Brothers Karamazov* in which Father Zosima differentiates it from romantic love. A troubled lady confesses that she has devoted her life to helping the poor and needy, yet she cannot bear being in the same room as a sick or filthy person. Hers was a romantic devotion to the glory of a noble cause, but she had little love for the wretched, sick, and poor. Victor Hugo likewise poignantly portrays unconditional love in *Les Misérables*, where the kindness of a priest turns a hardened criminal into a martyr who saves innocent lives.

The utilitarian essence of *ren* is reflected in reciprocity, i.e., benevolence begets respect and loyalty. This implies that Confucius saw *ren* as the pragmatic route to better human relations. This is not to debase the virtue of *ren*. On the contrary, it extols the wisdom of *ren* as virtuous behaviour that rewards perspicuous leaders.

Propriety as the sculptor of character

Li (礼) translates into rites, propriety, and decorum. In modern society, *li* has often been viewed as a stifling relic of feudal societies that demanded abject submission to authority. Subjects prostrated themselves before kings, and children were drilled in stiff decorum towards their elders. Lin Yutang, who understood Chinese culture better than most, found Chinese etiquette "too decorous, too correct."[19]

Confucian scholars generally agree that *ren* and *li* occupy pre-eminent positions among Confucian precepts, even though there has been an interesting debate over which was the core of Confucian thought.[20] How could mere propriety contend with something as fundamental as benevolence? A hint of this is provided in *Analects* 1.12:

> In the usages of ritual it is harmony that is prized. . . . Both small matters and great matters depend upon it. If things go amiss, he who knows harmony will be able to attune them. But if harmony itself is not modulated by ritual, things will go amiss.

Harmony or *he* (和) was, for Confucius, and indeed for most of Chinese philosophy, the ultimate goal of all ethics, i.e., harmony within the family; between ruler and subjects; among merchants, peasants, soldiers, and craftsmen; and between man and nature. Benevolence may be the moral base for social harmony, but without proper personal conduct, such harmony could not be achieved:

> If you do not learn the rules of Propriety, your character cannot be established. . . . If a man can for one day subdue himself and return to propriety, all under heaven will ascribe perfect virtue to him. Namely, only by controlling one's self and returning to the ritual system can benevolence be realized in the whole world.[21]

Most scholars conclude from this passage that propriety serves benevolence – the former is the branch and the latter is the root; the former is the form and the latter is the substance.[22] A closer look at the reality of human psychology reveals a more subtle relationship between rites and benevolence.

I am reminded of Singapore of the 1960s when Prime Minister Lee Kuan Yew introduced draconian laws in his haste to improve the social etiquette of Singaporeans. In the early days of the island's development, civic consciousness was low. People threw litter on the streets with abandon and spat in public places. A hefty fine of up to S\$500 was levied on as small a transgression as dropping cigarette ash on the ground. After one generation, the litter law still applies, but is hardly ever needed. People became accustomed to clean streets. Even in foreign places where no litter laws are in force, civic-conscious Singaporeans instinctively and dutifully look for trash bins to dispose of fast food packaging and mineral water bottles after consumption. Public cleanliness had become *internalized* as part of their character, somewhat like the way in which the Pavlovian dog internalized the sound of arriving food as the trigger for salivation. Transforming decorous conduct into heartfelt benevolence was among the deepest insights of Confucius as social psychologist.

Other Confucian virtues like righteousness (*yi*), loyalty (*zhong*), and filial piety (*xiao*) can, to a large extent, be subsumed under benevolence. For example, it has been argued that the pursuit of righteousness or justice must be motivated by benevolence. Loyalty is inspired by and also springs from benevolence to others, and filial piety is a source of benevolence towards one's parents.

At times, Confucian precepts come into mutual conflict. In periods of Chinese history when the emperor was cruel or incompetent, people abandoned loyalty to the throne and rose up in rebellion in the name of righteousness. In the great Ming classic *The Water Margin*, the battle cry of the brigands and fugitives from miscarriages of justice was *ti tian xing dao* (替天行道), meaning "Justice with the mandate of heaven." The Emperor appealed to the Confucian upbringing of their leader Song Jiang and persuaded them to lay down arms to seek conciliation. It was a trap and the group was decimated.

Family bonds and loyalty play uniting roles in family companies. These companies inherently face another kind of tension, that of balancing Confucian values and wealth-maximizing capitalism.

"Confucian capitalism" and family businesses

After Herman Kahn attributed the rise of the tiger economies of East Asia in the 1970s to a potent fusion of traditional Confucianism and liberal capitalism, much has been written about "Confucian capitalism."[23] It is a somewhat awkward term marrying two categories – a moral philosophy for social harmony and an economic system for maximizing wealth. Yao aptly characterizes the entrepreneurial success of Confucian capitalism as the "valorization" of the economic success of East Asian societies and their emphasis on Confucian values of collectivism and social humanism.[24] In regard to China, Yang sees it as the fusion of Confucianism, socialism and liberalism in the wake of the disastrous Cultural Revolution. He argues that although these enterprises retain a veneer of feudalism, any such connotation should be understood not as poor governance, but one that affirms the Confucian concept of *da yitong* (大一統), a common respect for authority to provide unity for the pursuit of the common good.[25]

Despite the steady spread of Western capitalism based on maximizing the wealth of enterprise shareholders, the family enterprise headed by an entrepreneurial patriarch remains the dominant model for successful companies in China and many East Asian countries. The family enterprise is in many respects a microcosm of ancient imperial administrative structures guided by Confucian precepts. Loyalty is prized as much as, if not more than, competence. Meritocracy plays the additional role of culling the best available talent to serve as employee managers, in much the same way that elite mandarins in ancient China were selected through competitive examinations and subsequent performance as officials. Succession is planned for the offspring of the patriarch, who is often – but not always – the eldest son (primogeniture), as in the case for succession to the throne in imperial China.

Two recent Harvard Business School case studies shed light on Confucian capitalism.

The CP Group

The Charoen Pokphand Group (CP Group) is a powerful sprawling conglomerate with interests in agribusiness and food, retail, and distribution, and telecommunications.[26] Founded in 1921, this Thai-Chinese group has extensive investments in China, and is led by Dhanin Chearavanont (whose Chinese dialect name is Chia Kok Min 谢国民), the youngest son of the company's founder. Chia grew up in Thailand, but his father ensured that he received part of his education in China, making him fluent in both Thai and Chinese.[27] When China opened up its economy in 1978, the CP Group was the first foreign investor in the country and the first foreign company registered in the special economic zone of Shenzhen, Guangdong province. Since then, the Chia Tai Group has been a famous name in Chinese industry.

The Chearavanont business philosophy values filial piety, fairness, and philanthropy. A believer in cultivating professional management, Chia handpicks senior managers to run the company while discouraging family interference in business operations. This allows the professional managers to run the business, while the family stays on high ground, guarding the group's values and laying down long-term plans. Wives, sisters, and daughters are kept out of the business in line with old Chinese values. Younger family members are required to start new businesses and prove their mettle before being admitted into management ranks.

The Confucian values of the patriarch have been the glue binding the ethics, business methods, and strategies of this successful overseas Chinese organization. At the same time, it allows meritocracy and competent professionals from outside the family space to contribute to the company's success.

Dasheng

Within mainland China, similar balancing of family values and professional management practices may be seen in large enterprises. Some of them have shown impressive durability, even though the methods employed are textured and vary with the social upheavals of the country.

Dasheng Cotton Mills was one such enterprise. Dasheng has survived for over a hundred years, transforming from a family-owned enterprise in the late Qing dynasty to a state-owned company in the twenty-first century, all while keeping its core culture remarkably intact.[28] The case is instructive as it does not fit the conventional model of Confucian capitalism in which an enterprise gradually absorbs Western capitalistic ideas over time to keep up with new challenges in a rapidly changing environment.

When Zhang Jian (Figure 2.2) started Dasheng in Nantong, Jiangsu province, he laid down rules on time discipline, the handling of company property and equipment, and employee conduct at work. Although his family did not own a majority of the shares, he exercised control through a complex holding structure. Dasheng benefitted from Zhang Jian's relations with the government and his acts of philanthropy. He was succeeded by his son who maintained good relations with officials. Brought up in the Confucian tradition, Zhang demonstrated concern for society by giving to schools, orphanages, libraries, and museums. In 1948, when the Communist Party's victory was imminent, Zhang's son and nephew chose to stay rather than relocate the business to Taiwan or Hong Kong.

FIGURE 2.2 Zhang Jian, founder of Dasheng[29]

Today, the company is a state-owned enterprise known as the Jiangsu Dasheng Group, and has over 10,000 employees. Its official website has a page dedicated to Zhang Jian. Although the family is no longer involved in the company's management, the founder's grandson Zhang Xuwu continues to cultivate political and social goodwill for the group.

Conclusion

When the young Confucius anguished over despotic rulers and restive citizenry in the Spring-Autumn period over 2,500 years ago, little did he know that the moral code he assembled and taught passionately for most of his lifetime would survive and thrive to the present day. Confucianism is pervasive in East Asia not just in family relationships, social harmony, and state governance, but also in the embedded culture of business corporations. Among its direct manifestations are social and business networks, which is the subject of the next chapter.

Notes

1 Lim, Rajah and Prasad (2012).
2 Huang (2014).
3 Unless otherwise stated, all references to *The Analects* in this chapter are from *The Analects of Confucius* (1999), translated into English by Arthur Waley and into Modern Chinese by Yang Bojun.
4 One of them was the literary luminary Laoshe, playwright of *Chaguan* (Teahouse) and many theatrical works of social satire that are now studied as classics of modern Chinese literature.
5 Allison (2018). Graham Allison coined the phrase "Thucydides's Trap" to refer to a situation when one great rising power threatens to displace another; war is almost always the end result. Allison based the phrase on the war that broke out when the ancient Athens rose in prominence and power to challenge Sparta's domination of ancient Greece.
6 Zhang (2014). Zhang's editorial article covers Xi Jinping's effusive praise of Confucianism at the International Conference commemorating the 2,565th anniversary of Confucius' birth. According to Zhang, Xi's speech, which opened the fifth Congress of the International Confucian Association in Beijing, acknowledges Confucius and his teachings thus: "Confucius . . . has profoundly influenced the Chinese civilization and has been an important part of traditional Chinese culture. . . . For thousands of years, Confucius has been regarded as a symbol of China's traditional culture, as well as the country's intellectuals. He was deified as a great sage in ancient China, and despised as a regressive pedant during the decade-long Cultural Revolution (1966–1976)." Zhang's editorial piece also points out that observers like Wang Xuedian, executive vice-president of the Advanced Institute of Confucian Studies of Shandong University, spoke up on the ways in which the ideology impacted Chinese society: "Chinese traditional culture, represented by Confucianism, can provide stable values to enhance social cohesion and sense of identity."
7 Jin (2014); Asia Society (2012).
8 Page (2015); Gardels (2014); Peng (2010).
9 Xinhua News Agency (2014).
10 Asia Society (2012).

11 See Billioud (2011); Billioud and Thoraval (2015). The "classical texts" to which Billioud allude are the ancient classics known as the "Four Books and Five Classics." They comprise Confucian texts as well as timeless classics like *The Book of Poetry* or *Sijing* (诗经) and *The Book of Changes* or *Zhouyi* (周易).
12 Nye and Goldsmith (2011); Nye (2011).
13 Permission to use this picture was granted by its owner Prof Sébastien Billioud, conveyed in an email dated 21 June 2019 to the author.
14 The Chinese character 仁 is made up of 人 (person) and 二 (two), signifying an affective relationship between two persons.
15 See *The Republic of Plato (1968)*, Book VII, translated into English by Allan Bloom.
16 Yang (1999), pp. 39–40.
17 See Fei (1992), Chapter 4.
18 *The Analects* (1999).
19 Lin (1936), p. 109. Lin's criticism of Chinese etiquette may be better understood by reading the passage bearing the following quote: "The middle-class morality of Confucianism has worked wonderfully for the common people, both those who wear official buttons and those who kowtow to them. But there are people who do not wear or kowtow to the official buttons. Man has a deeper nature in him which Confucianism does not quite touch. Confucianism, in the strict sense of the word, is too decorous, too reasonable, too correct. Man has a hidden desire to go about with dishevelled hair, which Confucianism does not quite permit." One cannot help detecting a certain partiality of Lin towards Daoism, which we shall discuss in Chapter 4 of this book.
20 Yang (1999), pp. 38–9.
21 Ibid., p. 45.
22 Ibid., p. 44.
23 Kahn (1979), Redding (1990).
24 Yao (2002), p. 5.
25 Yang (2007), cited in You (2017).
26 Kirby and Manty (2011).
27 Chearavanont (2016).
28 Koll (2008).
29 Picture from https://commons.wikimedia.org/w/index.php?curid=8051190.

References

Graham Allison. (2018). *Destined for War: Can America and China Escape Thucydides's Trap?* Boston, MA: Mariner Books.

The Analects of Confucius. (1999). Translated into English by Arthur Waley, and translated into Modern Chinese by Yang Bojun. Changsha: Hunan People's Publishing House.

Asia Society. (2012). "Understanding China and Its Rise: The Civilization-State," 31 July. Available online at https://asiasociety.org/india/understanding-china-and-its-rise-civilization-state. Accessed 21 April 2019.

Sébastien Billioud. (2011). "A Revival of Confucianism in China Today?" *French Network for Asian Studies*, March. Available online at www.gis-reseau-asie.org/en/revival-confucianism-china-today. Accessed 14 May 2019.

Sébastien Billioud and Joël Thoraval. (2015). *The Sage and the People: The Confucian Revival in China.* Oxford: Oxford University Press.

Dhanin Chearavanont. (2016). "Dhanin Chearavanont: The Thai company with Chinese roots and a global vision." *Nikkei Asian Review*, 1 September. Available online at https://asia.nikkei.com/Spotlight/My-Personal-History/Dhanin-Chearavanont/Dhanin-Chearavanont-1-The-Thai-company-with-Chinese-roots-and-a-global-vision2. Accessed 21 April 2019.

Fei Xiaotong. (1992). *From the Soil: The Foundations of Chinese Society, A translation of Fei Xiaotong's Xiangtu Zhongguo*. Translated by Gary G. Hamilton and Wang Zheng. Berkeley and Los Angeles, CA: University of California Press.

Nathan Gardels. (2014). "Xi Restores Confucianism As China's Ideology." *Huffington Post*, 18 December. Available online at www.huffpost.com/entry/xi-jinping-confucianism_b_5897680. Accessed 16 July 2019.

Huang Yanzhong. (2014). "The 2008 Milk Scandal Revisited." *Forbes*, 16 July. Available online at www.forbes.com/sites/yanzhonghuang/2014/07/16/the-2008-milk-scandal-revisited/#4a11168e4105. Accessed 14 February 2019.

Jin Kai. (2014). "The Chinese Communist Party's Confucian Revival: Xi Jinping's Emphasis on Confucius has a Modern-day Political Purpose." *The Diplomat*, 30 September. Available online at https://thediplomat.com/2014/09/the-chinese-communist-partys-confucian-revival/. Accessed 10 February 2019.

Herman Kahn. (1979). *World Economic Development: 1979 and Beyond*. London: Croom Helm.

William C. Kirby and Tracy Yuen Manty. (2011). "CP Group: Balancing the Needs of a Family Business with the Needs of a Family of Businesses." Harvard Business School Case 312–059, September. (Revised November 2011).

Elisabeth Koll. (2008). "Enterprise Culture in Chinese History: Zhang Jian and the Dasheng Cotton Mills." Harvard Business School Case 308–068, February. (Revised September 2010).

Vivien K.G. Lim, Rashimah Rajah and Smrithi Prasad. (2012). "Food for Thought: The 2008 China Milk Scandal." Case no. 9B12C047. London, Ontario: Richard Ivey School of Business Foundation.

Lin Yutang. (1936). *My Country and My People*. London and Toronto: William Heinemann. Available online at https://ia800309.us.archive.org/31/items/MyCountryAndMyPeople1936/MyCountryAndMyPeople1936.pdf. Accessed 13 February 2019.

Joseph S. Jr. Nye (2011). "Power Shifts." *Time*, 9 May. Available online at http://content.time.com/time/magazine/article/0,9171,2068114,00.html. Accessed 16 July 2019.

Joseph S. Jr. Nye and Jack Landman Goldsmith. (2011). "The Future of Power." *Bulletin of the American Academy of Arts and Sciences* no. 2 (Spring): 45–52. Available online at www.jstor.org/stable/i40050984. Accessed 10 February 2019.

Jeremy Page. 2015. "Why China Is Turning Back to Confucius." *Wall Street Journal*, 20 September. Available online at www.wsj.com/articles/why-china-is-turning-back-to-confucius-1442754000. Accessed 16 July 2019.

Peng Guoxiang. (2010). "Inside the Revival of Confucianism in Mainland China: The Vicissitudes of Confucian Classics in Contemporary China as an Example." *Oriens Extremus* 49: 225–35. Available online at www.jstor.org/stable/24047743. Accessed 22 September 2018.

Plato. (1968). *The Republic of Plato*. Translated with notes and an interpretive essay by Allan Bloom, 2nd edition. USA: Basic Books.

Gordon Redding. (1990). *Capitalism: Discourse, Practice and the Myth of Chinese Enterprise*. Berlin and New York: W. de Gruyter.

Xinhua News Agency. 2014. "China Commemorates Confucius with Ceremony." *China.org.cn*, 25 September. Available online at www.china.org.cn/china/2014-09-25/content_33608222.htm. Accessed 8 February 2019.

Yang Bojun. (1999). "Introduction." In Confucius, *The Analects*, translated into English by Arthur Waley and translated into Modern Chinese by Yang Bojun, pp.36–63. Changsha: Hunan Peoples Publishing House.

Yang Gan. (2007). 通三统, *Communication of the Three Traditions*. Beijing: Joint Publishing.

Yao Souchou. (2002). *Confucian Capitalism: Discourse, Practice and the Myth of Chinese Enterprise*. Oxford and New York: Routledge.

You Mi. (2017). "Chinese Globalization, Confucian Capitalism, and Transnationalism?" *Mezofera.org*, October. Available online at http://mezosfera.org/chinese-globalization-confucian-capitalism-and-transnationalism/. Accessed 17 July 2019.

Zhang Pengfei. (ed.) (2014). "China commemorates Confucius with high-profile ceremony." *Xinhua*, 25 September. Available online at http://english.cntv.cn/2014/09/25/ARTI1411604274108319.shtml. Accessed 1 March 2018.

3

RELATIONSHIP NETWORKS IN CHINESE BUSINESS

Each person should sweep the snow from his own doorsteps and should not fret about the frost on his neighbour's roof.[1]

(Old Chinese saying)

In his celebrated collection of essays, *From the Soil: The Foundations of Chinese Society*, Fei Xiaotong, widely regarded as the father of modern Chinese sociology, identifies "selfishness" as the most serious shortcoming of "country people" in China.[2] City people, too, suffer from the same social affliction, but even so rural China remains the fount of traditional Chinese culture.

Fei's hometown of Suzhou was noted for beautiful landscaped gardens and ancient canals that earned it the title of "Venice of the East." But to Fei, no waterway in the world was dirtier. This was because every home used the canals as public sewers with no consideration for the other families using the same water to wash their clothes and vegetables. "Why is this so?" Fei laments before telling us: "The reason is that such canals belong to the public. Once you mention something as belonging to the public, it is almost like saying that everyone can take advantage of it. Thus one can have rights without obligations."[3]

Egocentrism and Confucianism

Fei's portrayal of Chinese morality reveals a seemingly paradoxical nexus between selfishness and the moral precepts of Confucianism. This viewpoint stems from the intimate understanding of rural China which he acquired over a long personal journey of researching Chinese society.

Fei Xiaotong (费孝通) (1910–2005) studied sociology at Yenching University (which later merged with Peking University) after switching from medicine.

He had followed in the footsteps of the iconoclastic writer Lu Xun (1881–1936) who lamented that what ailed China was in the spirit, and it was that which had to be healed first.[4] He completed a doctoral thesis in 1938 at the London School of Economics under renowned anthropologist Bronisław Malinowski, who directed his attention to functional interrelationships within a community and to culture as viewed by members of that community.[5]

Fei's essays were written in the years just before and after the Chinese Communist Revolution of 1949. As an audacious young scholar early in the twentieth century, he challenged the received doctrine that viewed Chinese society in the Marxist dialectical framework. This framework comprised the class struggle of the proletariat against the bourgeoisie, ending in the triumph of an egalitarian society at "the end of history." Instead, he argued, the roots of social values lay in rural life where relationship networks provided safety nets in the harsh country landscape of droughts, pestilence, heartless landlords, and despotic rulers.

Relationships placed each person at the heart of his private network: selfishness was not in narrowly looking after his own interest above all else, but in placing the community closest to him – his family and his village comrades – at the centre of his life. The traditional Confucian Chinese was better described as *egocentric* rather than selfish.

Egocentricity characterizes a person who is totally selfless when making personal sacrifices for the good of his family and those closest to him in his relationship network. The American writer Pearl Buck, who grew up in China at the turn of the last century as a daughter of Christian missionary, poignantly depicted these enigmatic aspects of rural Chinese life in *The Good Earth*, a novel that helped her win the 1938 Nobel Prize in literature. But it took Fei's sharp insights to connect the struggles of rural folk with the values permeating Chinese culture to the present day.

To understand the nexus between Chinese culture and relationship networks, it is essential to delve further into Fei's core concept of egocentricity. With its emphasis on benevolence, ritual, justice, and loyalty, Confucianism might seem to be at odds with the kind of selfishness that Fei attributes to the Chinese individual. Yet, within the larger context of a person's community, there is indeed more compatibility than tension between Confucianism and selfishness.

The term "egocentrism" as used by Fei is translated from *zi wo zhu yi* (自我主义), which may be understood through a graphical depiction of a person's position within his community. Fei uses the analogy of a pebble thrown into a lake. When the pebble hits the water, concentric circles of ripples spread out, each ripple getting weaker as it spans a larger circle distant from the centre (see Figure 3.1). The relationships of kinship fundamental to Chinese society are represented by the ripples of enlarging circles.

At the centre is the individual self. His interests are focussed on the people closest to him in the most proximate circle. These interests diminish as he moves away from the centre to the ever larger circles. The next circle might be his comrades in the village, fellow disciples of a pugilistic master or a respected tutor, and distant relatives

FIGURE 3.1 Relationship networks like ripples in water[6]

acquired through marriages of his immediate family could occupy the circle after that.[7] Much further out are people from other villages. For most common folk, situated at a remote distance would be the emperor, feared and obeyed but best when far away, as captured by the aphorism *tian gao huangdi yuan* (天高皇帝远), meaning "The skies here are high here, and the emperor is far away."

The person who places the interests of his family, clan and close associates above all others does not appear selfish to those who enjoy his largesse, especially if he is a man of means. If his financial circumstances were not as fortunate, he might sacrifice his own comfort for that of his family. A filial son would forgo a promising career and stay home to look after aged parents. He could then be characterized as selfless, placing the interest of his closest community above his own.

Such behaviour coheres with the communitarian values, extolled by East Asian leaders, like Lee Kuan Yew, which place the community above self, and the group above the individual.[8] However, the community in Fei's model is narrowly confined to the closer circles, and the generosity of the individual may not include communities centred on other individuals.

Fei depicts Western society as comprising bundles of rice straws, each representing an individual. Several bundles are stacked together for transport. The straws, bundles, and stacks make up the haystack. The bundles that make up the haystack represent organizations in Western society. Or, as Fei puts it: "I want to indicate that in Western society individuals form organizations. Each organization has its own boundaries, which clearly define those people who are members and those who are not."[9]

Most pertinently, the relationship obligations within Chinese rural society are manifestations of Confucian precepts. Formal prescribed relationships known as *lun* (伦) arise from the Confucian ideals of benevolence, rites, and filial piety. Ancient texts describe *lun* as "the order existing in the ripples of water," and various components of *lun* express proper classifications and order.[10] The *Book of Rites* compiled in the Western Han period (206 BC–AD 8) spelt out ten *lun* of importance. Of these, the most cited in Confucian texts are *wulun* (五伦) or the five rites: the relationships between ruler and subject, father and son, husband and wife, older and younger brothers, and between friends. The practice of *lun* institutionalizes egocentric behaviour as societal norms of conduct.

The culture of *guanxi* in governance and management

The social relationships Fei describes are helpful in explaining relationship networks in Chinese society known as *guanxi* (关系). *Guanxi* has been part of the business and governance culture of the Chinese from ancient times. It persists not only on the Chinese mainland and Taiwan, but has endured in the present day amongst the sprawling Chinese diaspora in Southeast Asia.

Although Fei makes a passing mention of *guanxi* in *From the Soil* by treating it as a natural manifestation of social networks bound with cultural values, the extent and nature of *guanxi* networks in modern China have become far more extensive than what he might have envisioned eighty years ago. Loosely translated as "connections," *guanxi* is a complex network of assistance provided to facilitate transactions, mostly (but not exclusively) in a business context.

Guanxi is extensively documented in academic literature and business reports on China, and cultivation of *guanxi* for business is a staple of courses on Chinese business, even gaining the status of a minor academic discipline as "guanxilogy." Many books and case studies on the subject are eagerly lapped up by business neophytes wanting to engage China.

Guanxi in business involves such diverse manoeuvres as clinching a trade deal, being allocated a choice piece of land for development, or securing an appointment as a government official. In many instances, they border on corruption, with cash changing hands or gifts proffered in kind ranging from sexual favours to financing overseas education for an official's child. However, within the wider Chinese cultural tradition, such crass practices represent only the low end of a hierarchy of *guanxi* relationships, the highest of which encapsulate the noblest of Confucian ideals.

Confucian tradition expects the ethical man to fulfil his obligations to family, kinfolk, clan, and even to outer circles associates. A moral person does not forget his obligations to his family and community. Mencius, the most influential disciple of Confucius, was known to be willing to subordinate some common ethical principles to discharging obligations to those closest to him. Legend has it that he was asked how he would deal with the conflict between justice and filial piety if he was presiding over a trial where his father was charged with a capital crime.

He characteristically replied that he would move his father to another jurisdiction that would not pursue the case.

Mencius was also prepared to lie to his king if that was so required by higher moral considerations. In a lively exchange with fellow disciple Jinzi, the latter chided Mencius for being disrespectful to the King: "In the family there is the father-son relation, in society there is the ruler minister relation; these are the most important relationships. . . . I have seen the King respect you, but I have yet to see you respect the King!"[11] Mencius retorted that doing the moral thing was more important than abiding by the rules: "The great person is only concerned with doing what is appropriate."[12]

Egocentrism within Confucian culture means that each person puts his closest interests above those in the outer circles of relationships, and much above those not within his relationship network. Historically, it would be nothing out of the ordinary for a government official to help a relative or the son of his close comrade secure a good employment position or quietly gain a slight edge in securing a contract. Within many jurisdictions in Western society, such behaviour could be regarded as corruption or nepotism. In traditional Chinese society, however, the line between giving someone a nudge to gain advantage and corruption in a legal sense is blurred. It continues to be less than rigidly defined in contemporary China.

Guanxi continues to be pervasive in contemporary China. Chinese management operating within *guanxi* networks are guided by the Confucian values that underlie these relationships. In the examples and case studies illustrated in a later section, we see how varying shades of *guanxi* influence governance in business, state administration, and the management of human relationships in everyday life.

Bonds of brotherhood in war and business

An enduring form of *guanxi* derives from comradeship and bonds of brotherhood forged among people who have gone through life-and-death struggles together. The Ming classic *The Water Margin* has enthralled generations of readers with heroic exploits of fugitives from justice. Seeking refuge from corrupt officials who had manipulated an incompetent emperor, 108 stout-hearted comrades-in-arms or *haohan* lived together as brigands in the heavily fortified mountain called Liangshan in Shandong province. They relentlessly attacked imperial forces as vigilantes. Their leader, Song Jiang, was a Confucian scholar and a high official who had fallen victim to court intrigue and had fled to Liangshan, followed soon by many upright casualties of similar injustices. These included Wu Song, once head of the Imperial Guards, who killed a marauding tiger with his bare hands while in a furiously drunken state. He fell from grace after killing his brother's wife, the legendary Pan Jinlian (the Golden Lotus), who had poisoned her husband at the instigation of her wealthy merchant lover Xi Menjing. Xi's connections and generous gifts to court officials kept him protected from justice. Wu Song was snatched from the executioner's sword by the Liangshan brigands. There was also Lin Chong, former chief instructor of the military academy, who built a powerful army that struck fear in the emperor's forces. They pillaged and plundered the decadent rich at will, and waged a fearless guerrilla war against the throne.

The military strategies used in their protracted war were the stuff of legends that Chinese soldiers and scholars alike have revelled in recounting. Among the notable students of *The Water Margin* strategies was the revolutionary Mao Zedong. This classic was never far from his side, as he used this as a manual for his guerrilla campaign against the Japanese and later the Nationalist government of Chiang Kai-shek.[13]

The bonds of brotherhood among the brigands of Liangshan translate to *yiqi* (义气), an amalgam of *yi* (justice) and the warm sense of brotherhood or *qi* (气) born of their common struggles. Their battle cry, *ti tian xing dao* (替天行道), which translates to "Carry out the justice of Heaven," lent moral legitimacy to a common cause of justice and strengthened their brotherhood bonds. *Yiqi* is a source of long-term *guanxi*, the form most culturally true to Confucian ideals. People who have been comrades in battle, joined to combat injustice, or struggled together to build a successful organization, share bonds built on common ideals and forged in adversity. These comrades have entered the innermost circle of Fei's egocentric self, ranking virtually equal to family members.

Sometime in the 1990s, I had the privilege of attending a private talk to a small group of corporate chief executives given by the notable Malaysian tycoon Robert Kuok. In a small meeting room in his Singapore Shangri-La Hotel room, Kuok recounted how, some years after the Chinese Revolution of 1949, China suffered severe foreign exchange shortages as its economy spiralled downwards after the failure of the Great Leap Forward. Kuok was by then already a business tycoon whose skills in trading sugar had won him the popular title "Sugar King." Although a Malaysian by nationality, he had warm sentiments towards China, the land of his ancestors. When the Chinese government asked him for help, he went out of his way, travelling to Brazil and other countries, to make deals that resulted in the filling of foreign exchange coffers of the Chinese government. The Chinese government never forgot what Kuok did for them. His personal standing approaches that of patriot philanthropists like Tan Kah Kee of Singapore who helped finance China during its war of resistance against the Japanese. Kuok came to the rescue of China with no expectation of pecuniary gain. He could not then have foreseen that China would emerge decades later as a powerful economy under Deng Xiaoping. The *yiqi* developed between Kuok and the Chinese government officials has lasted for decades, and there is no doubt that the *guanxi* that came with it has served his sprawling business interests in China well.

The late Sir Henry Fok was a tycoon with a daring past that endeared him to the Chinese and eventually won him a place in Beijing's political inner sanctum. During the Korean War (1950–1953), Western powers imposed a trade embargo and a partial blockade of the South China Sea, choking off food and materiel supplies to Chinese forces in the north. Then in his twenties, Fok was in the transportation business and owned a large fleet of trucks and boats that he used to smuggle medical and weapon supplies to Chinese forces. In later years, during the rapid expansion of the Chinese economy, Fok amassed a fortune and operated one of the largest smuggling operations in China with impunity, much of it through the southern port of Shantou near Hong Kong. His activities were documented in a 1996 *Forbes* article, "The Smuggler with Guanxi."[14] He never sued the magazine, but went on instead to build one of the largest business empires in Hong Kong.

In 1986, Fok helped shipping magnate Tung Chee-hwa with a $120 million investment in Tung's financially strapped family company Orient Overseas (International) Limited. With the backing of Beijing, Tung became the first governor of Hong Kong, cementing Fok's family connections with China. *Guanxi* of the kind that began with a patriotic act of courage to render aid to China during some of the country's darkest days was destined to last for a long time. The connections that he built continued for his family beyond his passing in 2006. He was buried in Hong Kong with the Chinese national flag draped over his casket.

Relationship networks at Volkswagen

A more purposeful form of *guanxi* cultivation may be found in the success story of the German automaker Volkswagen AG (VW) in the Chinese market. In 1984, the company signed a one-billion Chinese yuan joint-venture agreement with a consortium of Chinese partners. The twenty-five-year Sino-German partnership known as Shanghai Volkswagen (SV), which had the German partner holding 50 percent of the equity, enjoyed special tax reliefs. Key senior management positions were strategically divided, with the joint venture headed by a Chinese chief executive and a deputy appointed by VW. A second joint venture was signed in 1990, resulting in the two plants on the mainland combining with a third located in Taipei to supply and distribute cars to the mainland Chinese market.

By 1995, SV was sourcing 88 percent of the value of an automobile from China. This was the outcome of developing a network of domestic component manufacturers. The Santana 2000 launched in 1995 had 89 percent locally sourced parts, an outstanding achievement considering that component suppliers in China were thirty years behind the West when the joint venture began.[15]

SV's achievements may be attributed to a holistic strategy that encompassed organizational structure, quality training, and marketing strategy, taking advantage of local knowledge of the Chinese partners. Most significantly, they developed good relationships with local suppliers of parts and components. New manufacturing employees underwent three years of on-the-job training, with time set aside for classroom instruction. The joint venture faithfully adhered to Chinese government guidelines to establish research and development facilities staffed mainly by locals working with German experts.

Volkswagen's accomplishments in China were the result of farsighted business strategies that nurtured and reinforced *guanxi* not only with their Chinese partners, but also between the joint-venture company, its suppliers, employees, and government regulators. In 2017, thirty-three years after its first foray into China, VW entered into a new joint venture with the Chinese automaker Anhui Jianghuai Automobile Company Limited (JAC). Each of the partners in the twenty-five-year joint venture hold a 50 percent stake in the new company, which will develop, produce, and market electric vehicles and mobility services.[16] This is a partnership of technological equals aiming to become a world leader in the future market for the ecologically friendly electric cars.

Case studies of relationship networks

The Roaring Dragon Hotel – a clash of management styles

Since the 1950s, the Roaring Dragon Hotel (RDH) had been a reputable premium guesthouse in China's southwest. Because it was known to be a good employer, working in the hotel was a much sought-after privilege. Its cosy peace was broken in 2002 when the RDH board hired European hotel consultant Hotel International (HI) to convert the old-fashioned provincial guesthouse into a five-star international luxury hotel.

Veteran general manager Tian Wen's management practices were a relic from the planned economy era of China. Even though China's dynamic new market economy had started to permeate into the southwest, he did not emphasize development and expansion. Jobs and salaries were secure "iron rice bowls"; and the work was light and came with generous fringe benefits. Some employees even read magazines and played card games during working hours. Anxious to move with the times, the provincial government decided to upgrade the hotel to international standards. Thus it was agreed in principle that HI would assume management control of RDH.[17]

HI decided that the transition to modern management required RDH to break its old *guanxi* connections with the travel agencies that had brought in customers. The hotel general manager Tian Wen, who had for decades assumed the role of a Confucian patriarch to employees, was redeployed to play a perfunctory liaison role between HI and the RDH board. Paul Fortune, the new general manager appointed by HI, arrived from England in April 2002 and moved quickly to change work culture. In particular, international marketing practices had to replace relationships between key employees, travel companies, and tour operators that brought business to the hotel. Fortune's team picked out exemplary employees to spearhead the transformation, whilst replacing the rest.

During the first phase of its conversion to a five-star hotel, an old section of the hotel was closed and replaced by a modern new wing. HI planned to bring in eight expatriate professionals to manage the takeover. Fortune felt confident that RDH's service skills would be world-class within two years. In the transition process, key employees with valuable *guanxi* networks were laid off.

These events set the scene for a brewing confrontation between old employees, led by the sidelined former general manager Tian Wen, and Fortune's foreign team and new local hires. Because of differences with the tour agent who had brought in most of RDH's business, their relationship was terminated. Tourist guest numbers plunged and business slowed to a crawl.

In mid-January 2003, HI's board in Europe received official notification from the local Chinese provincial government of its intention to terminate their joint-venture contract. Fortune and all of HI's expatriate management left, and Tian Wen was reinstated as general manager. Room occupancy levels improved almost immediately, and by the beginning of June, sixty of the retrenched employees had returned.

Surprisingly, the RDH board continued with the same modernization and upgrading plan laid out by HI. Although the services of Tian Wen and many of the older staff were retained, it was only for the transitional period. The new wing of the hotel attracted international tourists as new connections were made with tour operators and their international networks.

Several years later, the new RDH International had become a thriving five-star hotel. Armed with lessons learnt from the severing old networks and a newfound respect for the culture of personal networks, the hotel gradually developed a separate *guanxi* network. It cultivated relationships with new tour agents who brought up-market tourists and high-spending business travellers. Many of the older staff gradually retired or left for three-star state-run hotels. The new staff were not only well-trained, but also worked efficiently and diligently to the new ethic that HI had envisioned.

In retrospect, HI had the right ideas, but its lack of understanding of Confucian culture and *guanxi* disrupted the transformation process. The governance culture of transparency and equal treatment for all employees had been pushed aside with undue haste. The RDH board was able to implement HI's strategies successfully in the new reboot and train new employees in modern service methods because it had due regard for the hotel's traditional values.

Esquel – ancient culture in modern management

The story of Esquel shows how attention to *guanxi* and a public-spirited communitarian culture enhanced the company's success in China.

In 1995, two years out of business school and cutting her teeth in a New York investment banking, Marjorie Yang received an unexpected call from her ailing father. A filial daughter from a Confucian family, she seemed destined to helm the family company. She had not only received management and technology education at Harvard and the Massachusetts Institute of Technology (MIT), but also inherited three generations of family engagement and connections in the textile and garment business.[18]

Marjorie's maternal grandfather, Cai Shengbai, scion of a wealthy Zhejiang family, attended Tsinghua University before earning an engineering degree in the United States and returning to Shanghai in 1919 to marry the daughter of the owner of Meiya Silk Mills. Marjorie's father, Yang Yuan-loong, married Cai's daughter, and went on to study textile science in the United States upon his father-in-law's advice.

Following the 1949 Chinese Revolution, he moved to Hong Kong and founded the garment manufacturer Esquel. Yang's timing was impeccable. Deng Xiaoping had only recently launched sweeping economic liberalization reforms. In the early years, private companies were not allocated quotas for the US market, but Esquel circumvented the restriction by investing in garment factories in Southeast Asia and Taiwan, and exporting through them.

With the encouragement of economic advisor Goh Keng Swee from Singapore, China set up eighteen special economic zones in coastal regions to attract foreign investments. Yang seized this opportunity to establish a weaving mill in the Gaoming municipality of Foshan city in the Pearl River Delta, attracted by its educated labour and business-friendly leadership. Esquel offered good working conditions and studiously cultivated relations with the company's workers as well as municipal authorities. It even built a low-emission coal-fired power station to provide extra power for the area, a blessing in those days of frequent electricity brownouts.

Taking over as chairman in 1995, Marjorie Yang heeded her father's advice to compete on quality rather than price. Textile quotas worked to Esquel's advantage as these were based on number of pieces of garments rather than their value. Furthermore, Esquel's ownership of the supply chain of factories spread over Asia granted it flexibility in sourcing and manufacturing efficiency. One of Marjorie's first major decisions was investing US$100 million in cotton farms in Xinjiang province in western China to ensure a stable supply of best-quality cotton. "It was my turning point," Marjorie reminisced. "I was so taken by the vastness of the desert and mountains."[19] These farms also ensured a stable supply of premium cotton for high-end dress-shirts. The investment decision was ahead of its time, as the Chinese government had yet to pay attention to the less developed western provinces. As one of the largest foreign investors in Xinjiang, Esquel readily developed close relationships with local officials in this resource-rich region. The investment also created a vertical supply chain, with its own raw cotton from Xinjiang and fabric from mills in Gaoming, enhancing competitive advantage. Gaoming's proximity to Hong Kong also cut delivery time to markets.

As it entered the twenty-first century with its firmly established operations and supply chain, Esquel found that the domestic market was buoyant. As a result, it expanded its retail presence. It was largely successful in this, and had four PYE brand stores and seven Shirt Stop stores by 2011. Thus, Esquel demonstrated that China could become a world leader in the apparels industry, and that the "Made in China" label could be a mark of quality.

With the goal of mutual cooperation and mutual benefit, Esquel showed how the private sector could benefit both business and society. Its corporate social responsibility (CSR) strategy went beyond respecting the environment in the cultivation of raw materials. It experimented with using fewer pesticides and implemented drip-irrigation technology to save water, a precious resource in an arid region. Education and sponsorship programmes included helping HIV prevention, supporting children of AIDS-stricken families, educating college students, and building libraries and schools in the areas in which it operated. Its microfinance projects provided loans through local credit cooperatives and trained farmers in financial management.

In Gaoming, the company's CSR agenda steadily increased output to meet customer demand, while reinvesting profits in the improvement of employee working conditions. It had a wastewater treatment facility using modern technologies, and built its own low-emission high-efficiency coal-fired power plant. Fibres and cotton dust in its factories were filtered out to ensure clean air for staff.

In December 2006, Esquel was awarded a China Social Compliance Certificate, a crowning achievement of the company's CSR efforts and a reflection of the powerful *guanxi* Marjorie has developed with the government and the industrialists in China. Accolades continue to pour in. Esquel was named one of the top ten foreign enterprises in Guilin, Guangxi, in 2015; it received the prestigious Hong Kong Management Association (HKMA) Award for Excellence in Training and Development in 2016; and it won the HR Innovation Award from *Human Resources Magazine* in 2017.[20]

Marjorie personally maintains close links with the academic community, serving on the advisory boards of Tsinghua, Harvard, and MIT.

Conclusion

Connections and networking are, of course, not peculiar to Chinese business and governance. Old boy networks in Western societies play a similar role. But as Kevin Lo points out in a study comparing Chinese *guanxi* with Western networks, the practice is more subtle and deeply rooted in Chinese society, requiring patience and deeper cultural understanding to manage.[21] In contrast, connections in the West were more of a convenient avenue to gain business advantage or open doors. Lo's study indicates that connections in the West are built up more readily, but may also have shorter shelf lives. However, *guanxi* and connections do sometimes work effectively within the cultural practice of Western business, and are fitting subjects for further research.

In China, *guanxi* is founded on Confucian culture and inseparable from ethical traditions. For this reason, it would be unrealistic to see *guanxi* ever ceasing to be an important social and governance aspect of Chinese life. Instead, it should be leveraged to smooth working relationships and build mutual trust for better business outcomes, without lapsing into illegal corrupt practices.

Notes

1 This saying is 各人自扫门前雪，莫管他家瓦上霜 (*ge ren zi sao men qian xue, mo guan ta jia wa shang shuang*) in Chinese.
2 Fei (1992), p. 60.
3 Ibid., p. 60.
4 Ibid., p. 5.
5 Fei was persecuted during the Cultural Revolution (1966–1976), but later rehabilitated and appointed first president of the Chinese Society for Sociology. As a prolific writer

and professor of sociology at Peking University, he helped change the course of sociology studies in China. His collaboration with University of Chicago anthropologist Robert Redfield resulted in the publication of *China's Gentry*, which was a staple of American university courses on China for many years.

6 Picture from https://commons.wikimedia.org/wiki/File:Beaver_at_Meadowbrook_Pond,_ Seattle_14.jpg.

7 Fei (1992), p. 60. Fei used the somewhat awkward term *chaxugeju* (差序格局), translated as differential modes of association, to describe these concentric social circles.

8 Barr (2000), p. 315.

9 Fei (1992), pp. 61–2. Fei's analogy has its limitations. For example, a person can belong to different organizations, and each person would have to be represented by a different straw in each organization. Nevertheless, as a picturesque model of Western social structure, it presents a useful contrast to the concentric circles of Chinese society.

10 Some examples of these ancient texts on *lun* are *Shiming* (*The Interpretation of Names*) and *Shuo Lunzi* ("On Relationships") in *Shehui Yanjiu* (*Studies of Society*) by Pan Guangdan (1898–1967). These other works are cited and elaborated upon in Fei (1992), p. 65.

11 Mencius (2007), p. 282, cited in D'Ambrosio (2015), pp. 137–45.

12 Ibid.

13 Li (1994).

14 Doebele (1996), p. 161.

15 Luo (2007).

16 Volkswagen Aktiengesellschaft (2017).

17 Grainger (2008); Grainger (2017).

18 McFarlan (2009); McFarlan, Kirby and Manty (2007).

19 Ibid., p. 6.

20 Esquel Group (2019).

21 Lo (2012).

References

Michael D. Barr. (2000). "Lee Kuan Yew and the 'Asian values' debate." *Asian Studies Review* 24 (3): 309–34. Available online at https://doi.org/10.1080/10357820008713278. Accessed 17 July 2019.

Paul J. D'Ambrosio. (2015). "The Value of Falsity in the *Mencius*: Early Confucianism is not Consequentialism." *International Communication of Chinese Culture* 2 (2): 137–45.

Justin Doebele. (1996). "A smuggler with *guanxi*." *Forbes*, 18 November.

Esquel Group. (2019). "Awards and Certifications: 2004–2019." Available online at www. esquel.com/awards-certifications. Accessed 17 July 2019.

Fei Xiaotong. (1992). *From the Soil: The Foundations of Chinese Society: A Translation of Fei Xiaotong's Xiangtu Zhongguo*. Translated by Gary G. Hamilton and Wang Zheng. Berkeley and Los Angeles, CA: University of California Press.

Stephen J. Grainger. (2008). "The Roaring Dragon Hotel." Case no. 908M04. London, Ontario: Richard Ivey School of Business Foundation.

Stephen J. Grainger. (2017). "Roaring Dragon Hotel: A Second Attempt at Modernization." In Gary Johns and Alan M. Saks (eds.), *Organizational Behaviour: Understanding and Managing Life at Work*, 10th edition, 76–81. Ontario, Canada: Pearson.

Li Zhishui. (1994). *The Private Life of Chairman Mao*. London: Chatto and Windus.

Kevin Lo. (2012). "Chinese Guanxi and Anglo-American Networking." *Journal of International Management Studies* 7 (2): 216–23. Available online at www.jimsjournal.org/25% 20Kevin%20D.pdf. Accessed 17 July 2019.

Luo Yadong. (2007). *Guanxi and Business*. Singapore, New Jersey and London: World Scientific.

F. Warren McFarlan. (2009). "Esquel Group: Integrating Business Strategy and Corporate Social Responsibility (TN)." Harvard Business School Teaching Note 310–050, October.

F. Warren McFarlan, William C. Kirby and Tracy Yuen Manty. (2007). "Esquel Group: Integrating Business Strategy and Corporate Social Responsibility." Harvard Business School Case 307–076, February. (Revised November 2011).

Mencius. (2007). *Mencius* [孟子]. Beijing: Zhonghua Shuju.

Volkswagen Aktiengesellschaft. (2017). "Volkswagen Launches New Joint Venture for e-Mobility in China," June. Available online at www.volkswagenag.com/en/news/2017/06/China_joint_venture.html. Accessed 17 July 2019.

4

DAOISM AND MANAGEMENT

The best of all rulers is but a shadowy presence to his subjects. When his task is accomplished, the people all say, "It happened to us naturally."

(Laozi, Dao De Jing)

Daoism (Taoism) is a holistic philosophy, emphasizing man as part of nature, and the harmony of man with nature. It is of deep significance to governance. In corporate governance, it celebrates the virtue of flexibility and enhances the ability to deal with contradictions, such as situations in which legal and moral considerations are in conflict. In state governance, it advocates *yin* and *yang* forces as checks on each other whilst seeking harmony through the balancing of opposing interests and ideologies.

Confucianism may have provided a moral code for the Chinese civilization, but it was arguably the ancient holistic thought in Daoism that made the Chinese civilization's unique contribution to mankind. Daoism has been the wellspring of wisdom as it goes with the flow of nature in the cultivation of health, social harmony, and the subtler aspects of statecraft.

Origins of the Dao (道)

Daoism is generally believed to have been founded by the sage Laozi (Laotze/Lao Tzu) (circa 601–531 BC) during the Spring-Autumn period of the Zhou dynasty, and further expounded by Zhuangzi (circa 370–287 BC) in the Warring States period.

The earliest discourses on holism can be found in the *Book of Changes* or *The Yijing* (易经), sometimes Romanized as *I-Ching*. Written in the early Zhou period (circa 1000 BC), this classic details the observations of natural phenomena and the patterns of dialectical forces in nature. Regularities in nature and the harmony of man with nature form the basis of the principles of *yin* and *yang* – the two balancing forces in the cosmos. This naturalistic philosophy stands in contrast to Confucian ethics, which relies on rituals and character cultivation to create social harmony. Whereas Confucianism sought to tame human instincts through the inculcation of decorum and kindness, Daoists prefer to let nature take its course. Man must submit to the natural order of the universe, and choose the smoothest path to survival and self-fulfilment within it.

Laozi lived in the philosophically vigorous Spring-Autumn period of Western Zhou, when "a hundred schools of thought contended." But it was also a harsh world of despotic rulers and corrupt officials that made survival a challenge. By returning to nature and its flows, Daoism provided a spiritual haven from disciplinary ideologies like Confucianism and Legalism. Laozi was a reclusive figure who wrote little and only reluctantly relented, following pleas from his disciples, to put his thoughts in writing. He left behind a mere 5,000 words comprising a series of aphorisms, each pregnant with philosophical musing and mystical flourish, offering profound insights into the nature of man as well as his social and physical environment. These were later compiled as the *Dao De Jing* (道德经) or *Tao Te Ching*.

Over two centuries later, Laozi's most accomplished follower Zhuangzi (庄子) or Chuangtze (Figure 4.1) gave Daoism a mass following through brilliant allegories and lively Socratic dialogues. A consummate writer and a formidable debater, his

FIGURE 4.1 The mystical Zhuangzi[1]

essays flowed with the exuberance of lyrical poetry. Some of his works conjured vivid fantasy images, like the mythical giant roc in his classic *Xiaoyaoyou* (逍遥游), often translated into English as "Wandering in absolute freedom and abandon." With wings that spanned half the sky, the roc flew as swiftly as the wind over mountains and valleys, completely detached from the crassness of the material world. The flight of the roc symbolizes liberation from the shackles of society, and the attainment of spiritual ecstasy that eludes the rich and famous.

Generations of scholars and commentators have drawn lessons in the philosophy of life from *Xiaoyaoyou*. Zhuangzi has been regarded as the first Chinese philosopher to extol the personal freedom of an "unrestrained rampant life"; and as his *Xiaoyaoyou* breaks through the limits of material form, it creates a "vast world without boundaries but also spiritual freedom without bondage."[2] Zhuangzi's fantasy story was so widely read that its title was adopted by Chinese medicine practitioners as the name of a common potion (*Xiaoyaosan*) for alleviating anxiety.

Zhuangzi's emphasis on detachment from the material world through the emptying of one's mind and allowing it to wander freely bears some resemblance to the calm and emptiness in Buddhist meditation. Indeed, it has been postulated that Zen Buddhism was the result of merging meditation with Zhuangzi's wandering at ease.[3]

Neo-Daoism

Given its advocacy of personal freedom without bondage to ruler and family, it was little wonder that Daoism was treated with deep suspicion after Confucianism had established itself as the state ideology in the Han dynasty (206 BC–AD 220). During the four centuries of the dynasty, Daoism quietly spread among intellectuals and common folk who took respite in it from the rigours of Confucian rites. Following the fall of Han, the 360 years of the Wei-Jin North-South dynasty (魏晋南北朝) saw, in a string of despotic rulers, political instability and life that was harsh and brutish. Commoners consequently sought a more comforting ideology, and found the free spirit of Daoism. Neo-Daoism arose from among these people, and a group emerged whose prolific output of essays, poetry, and music reinvigorated Daoist thought. These Neo-Daoists looked at Daoism through "cosmological Confucian lenses."[4] Steeped in Confucian learning, they rebelled against it, whilst incorporating some of its cosmological models like the Five Phases or *Wuxing* (五行) in their interpretation of classic Daoist texts.[5]

A group of talented and charismatic scholars in the Jin period, known as the Six Sages of the Bamboo Grove (Figure 4.2), spent much of their lives in the quiet of bamboo groves, engaging in philosophical discourse, wine, and music, and producing some of the most enchanting writings on Daoist philosophy of life. The outstanding figure among them was Ji Kang, who excelled in essay writing, poetry and music, and practised medicine.[6] His talents were spotted by the Emperor, who invited him to enter the elite administrative service. Ji Kang declined, writing a stinging letter to the emperor's emissary about the tedium and futility of being a Confucian official. This resulted in his tragic execution. China lost not only a great

FIGURE 4.2 The Seven Sages of the Bamboo Grove[7] (Ji Kang plays the zither)

Daoist thinker, but also the musical score of *Guangling san* (广陵散), a legendary piece of ethereal music composed by Ji and played with poignant calm at his execution. The musical score of *Guangling san* is lost, and many of Ji's followers have tried to recreate it centuries after his death.[8]

Concepts in Daoist philosophy

Dao

As the central concept in Daoist philosophy, "dao" is translated as "the way," with a normative nuance, indicating the correct path to take. While its centrality in Chinese thought is comparable to "truth" and "being" in Western philosophy, "the way" is more elusive.

The *Dao De Jing* begins with the enigmatic line "The Way that can be told is not an Unvarying Way" (道可道, 非常到), implying that the way can only be known or discerned but not talked about. It is reminiscent of the early Wittgenstein's concluding proposition in *Tractatus Logico-Philosophicus*, "What we cannot speak about, we must pass over in silence."[9] Despite their own warnings that the subject could not be talked about, both Laozi and Wittgenstein devoted their philosophical tracts to talking around it.

Yin and yang

There are extensive discussions of *yin* and *yang* in the *Yijing*, but it was the Daoist philosophers who gave it full expression in poetry, metaphysics, medicine, and the philosophy of life. The ideas of *yin* and *yang* reflect a dialectical logic that attempts to explain relationships and change. Stripped to its bare essentials, *yin* and *yang* are not much more than labels capturing the perception of duality in nature – light versus darkness, hardness versus softness, male versus female. Thus, the *yin-yang* doctrine is a holistic view of the world that places all entities as parts of a cosmic whole. These entities cannot have existence independent of their relationships to other entities. Dualism implies that an attribute like brightness has meaning only relative to darkness, much in the same way that beauty is relative to ugliness. As the *Dao De Jing* puts it, "It is because everyone under Heaven recognizes beauty as beauty that the idea of ugliness exists. Being and non-being grow out of one another; difficult and easy complete one another; long and short test one another."[10]

Objects and states can be similarly classified: day and night, summer and winter, hard and soft. Attributes come in contrasting pairs: male and female, hard and soft, rigid and yielding:

Yang	*Yin*
Strong	Mellow
Bright	Dim
Rigid, unyielding	Flexible, yielding
Hard	Soft
Transparent	Unfathomable
Hot, dry	Cool, moist
Fast, hurried	Slow, patient
Analytical	Discursive
Sensitive	Insensitive

The symbol of *yin* and *yang* (Figure 4.3) depicts their mutual dependence, as well as mutual restraint. They wrap around each other and keep each other company, while constantly checking one another so as to maintain balance.

FIGURE 4.3 The symbol of *yin* and *yang*[11]

Wuwei

Wuwei (无为) has been interpreted in various ways by Daoist scholars. *Wu* means non-existence, the absence of, or the prescriptive "eschew, avoid." *Wei* has many meanings in the Chinese language, of which the most relevant here is "to take action."[12] *Wuwei* thus means avoiding or restraining oneself from taking action in a situation: "Therefore the Sage relies on *actionless* activity, carries on wordless teaching. But the myriads of creatures are worked upon by him. . . . He rears them, but does not lay claim to them, controls them, but does not lean upon them, achieves his aim, but does not call attention to what he does."[13]

In a celebrated essay titled "Essentials for Keeping Good Health" (养生主), Zhuangzi illustrates *wuwei* by telling us about a butcher who carves up an ox like a consummate artist, acting throughout by intuition.[14] Commentators have conjectured that Zhuangzi's essay was a satirical swipe at Confucianism, with the Daoist butcher carving the rigid carcass of the Confucian ox.[15]

Holism, *yin-yang*, and the structure of thought

Holism and *yin-yang* balance are at the core of Daoist thought. They have had profound influences on social values, state governance, and corporate management in Eastern societies.

Yin-yang in management

Principles governing the dynamic relationship between *yin* and *yang* have proved useful in explaining social phenomena and medicine, and have found applications in management as well. One of the most basic principles is the notion that *yin* and *yang* oppose each other, but are also interdependent. It might sound paradoxical for two opposing forces to depend on each other for their existence, but contradiction is precisely at the heart of this holistic philosophy.

In political contention, the presence of an opposition to keep the ruling party on its toes is a fundamental precept of liberal democracies. However, as claimed by political scientists in the last two decades, some democracies in the West have become dysfunctional. This is apparent in the frequent gridlock between the American Congress and the presidency, and the recent shambles vis-à-vis Britain's planned departure from the European Union.[16] Yin and yang have not been kept in balance.

On the other hand, some Eastern democracies have found a way to combine an authoritarian executive branch of government that is built on a legislature put in place by free elections. Singapore has often been held up as such an example, as it is a successful nation with a government chosen by free elections. But this same government, which has won landslide victories in every election since it gained power in 1959, has such a strong grip on the national levers of power that it can confidently make economic plans decades in advance and push through tough long-term policies without fear of loss of power. The *yang* of free electoral democracies is finely balanced against the *yin* of the authoritarian governance.

In the management of organizations, tension commonly occurs between rigid, rule-based, transparent managers and those who would have rules bent or broken when the situation requires it. A healthy balance between the two kinds of management styles imbues the organization with the flexibility to deal with unanticipated situations that rules cannot adequately cover. In Eastern societies, the extensive operation of *guanxi* or connections in business represents the influence of *yin*, which grants an advantage to those you trust more because of relationship bonds. However, the influence of *guanxi* has to be moderated by *yang* forces that call for fair competition as guided by commercial considerations.

The transparent and rigid application of rules in an organization can work well when the business environment is stable and there are few unforeseen sudden changes in competition or technology. Predictability makes for more consistent management policies and results. On the other hand, the quick onslaught of disruptive technologies and the sudden emergence of a powerful competitor during times of turbulence may result in the organization putting aside some of the rigorous application of rules and policies in favour of the creativity and daring of its more entrepreneurial management members.

Nokia is an example of a company that was a stable and steadily growing dominant player in the mobile market until Apple, and then Samsung, burst onto the scene with the smart phone. Nokia's management, which can be considered too *yang* on account of its status as the dominant industry player for decades, lacked the flexibility to cope with the disruptive technology of smart phones.

Peoples of different cultures may be classified into *yin* types and *yang* types. Westerners are by and large *yang*, as they are transparent and inflexible in their beliefs. In contrast, the subtle and yielding people of the East are *yin*. There is also the enigmatic principle that one will find *yang* in *yin*, and *yin* in *yang*. In practice, this happens to varying degrees. Some Westerners like the French are considered to have more *yin* than most others, as they are hard for the *yang* Germans and English to figure out. Likewise, the East is mostly *yin*, although Japan is considered the most *yin* among the *yin* because they are more inscrutable and unfathomable than the rest. The feisty Koreans, on the other hand, are considered the *yang* among the *yin*.

While the Chinese are *yin* people, they do possess some strong *yang* characteristics. Historically, they have demonstrated this in their propensity to abandon quiet, unyielding submission for violent revolution. This is unsurprising given that the *yin* of pugilistic *taiijquan* can be turned into lethal *yang* blows in *kung fu*.

Structure of thought

The social and cultural practices of contemporary East Asians resemble those of the Chinese in antiquity, while those of modern Europeans can be traced back to the ancient Greeks.

Like the Chinese, many other East Asians are more likely to view the world in holistic terms than their Western counterparts. They are more sensitive to the environments and backgrounds against which events occur, and they appear more skilled in observing the ways in which events are intertwined and influence one another. This may have a great deal to do with the influence of Daoism. Through the principles of *yin-yang* in Daoism, the Eastern thought process is more holistic and more naturally inclined to seeing the bigger picture. As such, it is able to better navigate between contradictions and find a middle path between them.

In a study of international and American students at the University of Michigan, Nisbett detected cognitive differences between East Asians (including Koreans) and Americans.[17] He found that Americans focussed more attention on objects, and Easterners paid more attention to environment. He also discovered Easterners were more likely to recognize relationships among objects and events than Americans. For example, they were shown a picture bearing the images of a chicken, a patch of grass, and a cow. They were then asked which should be placed in the same group as the cow – the chicken or the grass. When viewing Figure 4.4, most Americans chose the chicken (as both are animals), but Easterners usually chose grass as the cows graze on grass.[18]

In 1991, Gang Lu, a Chinese national who was a physics doctoral student in the University of Iowa, shot and killed four people, including two of his professors. The Western media reacted by examining his psychological profile for clues of congenital insanity.[19] By contrast, the Asian media outlets studied his living conditions, the people with whom he associated and the aspects of his upbringing, searching for signs of social rejection that might have left psychological scars. There was also

FIGURE 4.4 Is the cow associated with the chicken or with grass?[20]

speculation that he was enraged at not receiving a dissertation prize that would have helped him get a job back in China.[21] The Eastern approach looked at the social support environment and events which may have alienated him and fuelled his resentment against those around him. The Western approach was forensic and reductionist, looking for a specific underlying cause.

Following China's much lauded hosting of the Olympics in Beijing in 2008, a partly fictional Hollywood movie, *Dark Matter*, offered a closure of sorts to the case. It conjectured that China's century of humiliation at the hands of the West, starting from the Opium Wars, had left psychological scars on the Chinese psyche, and these surfaced in Gang Lu as feelings of persecution and discrimination when he was in US society.[22]

Managing contradictions

To attain harmony, the Chinese instinctively seek compromise. As a result, East Asians appear more able to handle contradictions than Westerners. In dealing with disputes, a common approach is to find a middle way, accepting that each party has a claim on the truth and finding a position which both can accept. This may entail accepting contradictions and reaching a compromise via dialectics.[23]

The dialectic evolved in Chinese thought from the *Yijing* and the *Dao De Jing* with *yin* and *yang* negating each other to arrive at a higher level of existence.[24] This involves reconciling and transcending contradictions. It allows one to use the dialectic to persuade someone else to move closer to one's position, without necessarily resorting to abstract logic.[25] Dialectic can be interpreted as a basis for the principle of the Golden Mean, by which one finds a middle ground that accepts the coexistence of two extremes and balances them. One such example is Deng Xiaoping's innovative "one country, two systems" idea through which Hong Kong is accommodated within China. This compromise allows Hong Kong's free press and laissez faire economy to coexist with the limited freedoms and the planned economy of the mainland.

The practice of *guanxi* among the Chinese is riddled with contradictions. On the one hand, it is ethical behaviour arising from the deep bonds shared among people in the same inner group, such as family, clan, or martial arts brotherhood. On the other hand, it involves unethical favouritism, a soft form of corruption.

Contradictions exist in personal lives, as in the case of the great Tang poet Wang Wei, a Confucian intellectual and official in the emperor's administration. Away from the imperial court, he roamed as a free spirit in the mountains. His split personality was immortalized in the line *shen zai chaoting, dan xin cun shanye* (身在朝廷, 但心存山野), which means "His head in the imperial court, his heart among the vales and mountains."

In Chinese medical theory, even the nature of *qi*, the ubiquitous force in the human body that drives all physiological processes, is enigmatic. It behaves like energy, but is also a substance stored in the vital organs. Chinese cosmology made no clear distinction between matter and energy. In a sense, it was ahead of its time, awaiting Einstein's scientific breakthrough proving the mutual convertibility of matter and energy through the equation $e=mc^2$.

Various empirical studies lend support to the existence of cognitive differences between East Asians and Westerners arising from their differing abilities to handle contradictions. One study found that contradictory "self-knowledge" was more common among the Chinese and Japanese than Westerners.[26] East Asians also exhibited a higher degree of changeability in their self-beliefs. The study concluded that East Asians and Westerners searched for self-coherence within their cultures differently – where East Asians strove for balance, Westerners fixated on internal consistency.[27] A similar comparative study of Australians and Japanese suggest that East Asians' balancing of contradictions may serve the same function as Westerners' internal consistency.[28] In other words, Easterners are more likely to seek the middle way when confronted with contradictions, while Westerners focus on determining the veracity of one belief over another.

During the American Revolution, Patrick Henry declared, "Give me liberty or give me death."[29] A Chinese might have said he would have to be alive to enjoy liberty, and that he would be willing to give up half of his freedoms as a compromise. As liberal democracy and freedoms are prized in America, Americans would readily reject authoritarian leadership styles and a rigorously regulated press, and be prepared to pay the cost of freedom with a more disorderly society with less personal security and the need to bear firearms. But in the East where higher priority is placed on social harmony, the peoples are more willing to compromise by accepting benign authoritarian leadership that places prudent restraints on democratic institutions and press freedoms.

Personal and collective agencies

Compared with the Chinese, the ancient Greeks had a remarkable sense of personal agency – they were in charge of their own lives, and were free to act as they chose. This promoted a strong sense of individual identity. The Chinese, by contrast, exhibited a sense of *collective* agency. Their ultimate goal was harmony. In pursuit of this, each person was a totality of the roles he lived in relation to others.[30]

Lloyd sharply captured the contrast between the Chinese and Greek philosophies of science by deeming the greatest Greek scientific attainment to be the *invention* of nature, as if man stood apart from nature to understand and control it.[31] The Chinese, on the other hand, saw man as part of nature because the world consisted of continuously interacting substances. This oriented them towards the complexities of the context and environment, leading them to focus on relationships within nature. Instead of trying to tame or change nature, they sought the best way to be part of its flows and variations.

The Greek tendency to decontextualize led to the development of the study of logic, focussing on the structure of statements rather than their meanings. The Chinese developed dialecticism, which uses contradiction to understand relations among objects or events, and to transcend or integrate opposites such as *yin* and *yang*.

Holism in Chinese thought extends to the natural sciences. Ancient Greeks and their cultural heirs in the West saw the world in discrete atomistic terms that are separate from their environments; they felt themselves to be personally in control of events. East Asians are inclined towards the big picture, viewing objects in relation to their environments and events in relation to other events. Aetiology in Western medicine is reductionist, seeking a causative agent for the disease, such as a germ, abnormal gene, or a tumour.[32] In traditional Chinese medicine, disease is an expression of underlying disharmony in the body, and treated by restoring balance and natural flows.[33]

Wuwei: going with the flow as management strategy

The wisdom of *wuwei* was extended by Daoist scholars to widely varied areas, from the cultivation of life to the practice of statecraft. The underlying management principle is maintaining little or no intervention, going instead with the flow of forces that have been nurtured to lead us in the optimal direction.

The organizational leader is a Sage, who "nurtures creatures under his influence," setting the framework for them to do the right things in accordance with his vision. In practice, application of this principle does not necessarily imply total impassive inaction. One could take a step back and watch natural forces play out, knowing when to give a gentle nudge to take advantage of these natural flows to achieve one's objectives.

Daoism has inspired a leadership style called "actionless management" or *wuwei erzhi* (无为而治). Laozi speaks of the leader who breeds "myriad creatures" without leaning on them to do as he wishes. In modern management parlance, that would be the strategy of defining and developing the culture of an organization. Once the culture is in place, the leader only keeps a watchful eye over it. He assumes the role of the subtle and unseen Sage who "puts himself in the background; but is always to the fore; remains outside but is always there."[34]

The Sage is virtually the disembodied spirit of the organization, rarely seen or heard. But his presence is always felt, as he exerts influence quietly through forces within the organization that he has studiously cultivated and put in place. The wise leader of the organization does not pursue personal goals. Instead, he enhances and reinforces initiatives and processes within the organization. He does so without appearing to be striving for public recognition or financial reward, as he follows the precept: "Is it not just because he does not strive for any personal end, that all his personal ends are fulfilled?"[35]

By encouraging a shared culture in the organization with all going with the flow, the leader's aspirations and intentions are at one with those of his people. He tries to understand them first, rather than have them understand him. In turn, as his thinking aligns with the sentiments and sincere aspirations of members of the organization, their hearts are aligned. This is because "the sage has not a heart of his own, he uses the heart of the people as his heart." When things do not go his way, the leader, as the Sage, must know when to let go. If a project has gone wrong and there is little hope, the Sage does not try to save it. Instead, he lets it go. Hence, the sage's way is to act without striving.

Wuwei has been interpreted and adapted in various ways for management applications, and there is indeed a rich array of literature on this strategy by practitioners and researchers.[36] Chinese executives often practise *wuwei* intuitively. For example, a study of Chinese bankers observed that they practise *wuwei* as a reflexive process by being effectively present and participating instead of forcing the situation. People in the situation are aware of who they are, and by reflection, they see themselves as part of the flow. *Wuwei* also allows the participant to mitigate his personal risk by being part of the team flow.[37]

Among the most noted management practitioners of Daoist philosophy is the charismatic Jack Ma Yun.

Jack Ma and Daoism at Alibaba.com

The online retail giant Alibaba.com is now seen as China's rival to Amazon.com. But before Alibaba's founder Jack Ma (Figure 4.5) became its chairman, he was a humble schoolteacher and tour guide. Ma himself is widely acknowledged as a visionary leader, able to bridge "a social mandate with business sensibilities."[38] His favourite philosophical work is the *Dao De Jing*. His biographer has revealed that he carries it with him, frequently citing from it to employees and at international conferences.[39] Daoist philosophy permeates Alibaba corporate culture, which is fluid like the Daoist *yin* in coping with change, and *yang* in the transparency of

FIGURE 4.5 Jack Ma of Alibaba.com[40]

its corporate standards and strategies. Its corporate culture is also holistic in that it views the company as merely a part of a larger organic universe comprising customers, employees, society, and shareholders.

The *Dao De Jing* subtly embodies these characteristics. For example, it celebrates governing with the fluidity and depth of water: "The highest goodness resembles water. . . . It is similar to the Dao, dwelling with the right location, feeling with great depth, giving with great kindness, speaking with great integrity, governing with great administration, handling with great capability."[41]

Advocating Daoist inaction yet known to run a company with aggressive market strategies, the enigmatic Ma also infuses his people with a fighting spirit that is drawn from his love for Chinese martial arts, better known as *kung fu*.[42] His nickname "Feng Qingyang" is derived from the name of a legendary reclusive hero who personified the *kung fu* code of ethics that prized righteousness and the bond (*yiqi*) among members of a pugilistic clan.[43] Aspects of *kung fu* are inspired by Daoist methods of health cultivation, involving breathing techniques and the building of the body's internal strength to counter power punches of opponents.[44]

Jack Ma's management style emphasizes the team spirit that is cultivated through a philosophy of trust in the team, in keeping with *wuwei*: "The best of all rulers is but a shadowy presence to his subjects. . . . Hesitant, he does not utter words lightly. When his task is accomplished and the work done, the people all say, 'It happened to us naturally'."[45]

Notes

1 Picture source: https://commons.wikimedia.org/wiki/File:玄門十子圖_莊子.jpg.
2 See Yang (1999), pp. 53–4; Chen (2016), Chapter 1.
3 Yang (1999), p. 56.
4 Hansen (2017).
5 Ibid.
6 For an analysis of Ji Kang's philosophy of *yangsheng,* see Hong (2007).
7 Picture by author.
8 See also the section titled "Ji Kang and Ruan Ji: The Ethics of Naturalness" in Chan's (2019) entry on Neo-Daoism in the *Stanford Encyclopedia of Philosophy*.
9 Wittgenstein (2001) [1921], p. 89.
10 Lao Tzu (1997).
11 Picture by author.
12 See Hansen (2007) for an interesting analysis of the grammatical and lexicographic nuances of *wei*.
13 Lao Tzu (1997).
14 See Zhuangzi (1999), Chapter 3.
15 Cook (1997) cites a conjecture in this vein by noted writer Guo Moruo in 1944.
16 Karim (2019); Matthijs (2016).
17 See Nisbett (2003), Chapter 6.
18 Ibid.
19 Myers (1991).
20 Picture was constructed by author following a similar illustration in Nisbett's *Geography of Thought*, p. 141. Pictures of the animals are from https://commons.wikimedia.org/wiki/File:Rooster_Drawing.jpg; https://commons.wikimedia.org/wiki/File:Brown_Cow_Drawing.jpg; https://commons.wikimedia.org/wiki/File:Zoysia_matrella.jpg.

21 Kilen (2016); Plaza (2015), pp. 370–3.
22 Schell (2008).
23 "Dialectic," according to the Cambridge English Dictionary, is "a way of discovering what is true by considering opposite theories." It is a philosophical argument that involves a *contradictory* process between opposing sides. See Cambridge English Dictionary Online, (n.d.), "Dialectic." The classic dialectic was used by Greek philosopher Plato in the form of fictitious dialogues between Socrates and his interlocutors, who express views that Socrates challenges. The back-and-forth debate produces a progression to the more sophisticated position held by Socrates. Hegel's Dialectics, on the other hand, as explained by Maybee (2017) in the *Stanford Encyclopedia of Philosophy*, comprise three stages: a thesis of an idea, a reaction or antithesis to that the thesis, and a final synthesis when differences are resolved.
24 Nisbett, Peng, Choi and Norenzayan (2001), p. 294 opine that: "The Chinese dialectic includes notions resembling the Hegelian dialectic of thesis-antithesis-synthesis and finds its counterpart in modern 'post-formal operations' in the Piagetian tradition – for example, understanding of part-whole relations, reciprocal relations, contextual relativism, and self-modifying systems." Karl Marx and Friedrich Engels' *Die deutsche Ideologie* [The German Ideology], on the other hand, expressed contradiction in the form of dialectical materialism, which China officially adopted as an ideology from the time of Mao, although it appears not to have taken root. According to Francis Soo (1981), p. 91, Mao's *magnum opus* "On Contradiction" draws from his roots in ancient Chinese thought, and found expression in the adoption of his form of dialectical materialism.
25 Lloyd (1990), p. 119.
26 Spencer-Rodgers, Boucher, Mori, Wang and Peng (2009).
27 Ibid.
28 Using the concepts of naive dialecticism (i.e., the tendency to tolerate contradiction) and psychological essentialism (i.e., the tendency to attribute a fixed essence to something) as different aspects of consistency perception, Tsukamoto, Holland, Haslam Karasawa, and Kashima (2014) identify and compare patterns of perceived consistency of the self and national ingroup among Japanese and Australians. The Japanese showed more naïve dialecticism and less psychological essentialism for the self than did Australians.
29 "Give me liberty or give me death," Wikipedia. https://en.wikipedia.org/wiki/Give_me_liberty,_or_give_me_death! Accessed 20th May 2019.
30 Nisbett (2003), pp. 1–6.
31 Lloyd (1991), pp. 417–34.
32 See, for example, Brigandt and Love (2017).
33 See Hong (2016).
34 Lao Tzu (1997).
35 Ibid.
36 Cheung and Chan (2005); Johnson (2000); Sönmez (2015, 2019).
37 Xing and Sims (2011). "Reflexivity" in general is defined as "the fact of someone being able to examine his or her own feelings, reactions, and motives (= reasons for acting) and how these influence what he or she does or thinks in a situation." See Cambridge English Dictionary Online, (n.d.), "Reflexivity."
38 Su, Bansal and Laughland (2017), p. 3; and Wulf (2010).
39 Ybanez (2015).
40 Picture source: https://commons.wikimedia.org/wiki/File:Jack_Ma_Yun,_Tianjin,_2008_(cropped).jpg.
41 This quote from D.C. Lau's (1963) translation of the *Dao De Jing* was cited by Christopher B. Nelson (2015). I have extracted the relevant portions and edited them with prose punctuation.
42 *Financial Times* (2013).
43 For a detailed discussion on *yiqi*, see Chapter 3 of this book.

44 See Fingarette (1972), pp. 4–6; Ni (2010). The American philosopher Herbert Fingarette went so far as to romanticize it to a mystic level, calling it "[T]he magical but distinctively human dimension of our practicality," involving effects "produced effortlessly, marvellously, with an irresistible power that is itself intangible, invisible, unmanifest."
45 Lao Tzu (1963), cited in Custer (2016).

References

Ingo Brigandt and Alan Love. (2017). "Reductionism in Biology." In Edward N. Zalta (ed.), *Stanford Encyclopedia of Philosophy*. Stanford, CA: Stanford University. (First published on 27 May 2008). Available online at https://plato.stanford.edu/archives/sum2017/entries/zhu-xi/. Accessed 17 March 2019.

Cambridge English Dictionary. (n.d.). "Dialectic." *Cambridge Dictionary Online*. Available online at https://dictionary.cambridge.org/dictionary/english/dialectic. Accessed 14 March 2019.

Cambridge English Dictionary. (n.d.). "Reflexivity." *Cambridge Dictionary Online*. Available online at https://dictionary.cambridge.org/dictionary/english/reflexivity. Accessed 14 March 2019.

Alan Chan. (2019). "Neo-Daoism." In Edward N. Zalta (ed.), *Stanford Encyclopaedia of Philosophy*. Stanford, CA: Stanford University. (First published on 1 October 2019). Available online at https://plato.stanford.edu/archives/sum2019/entries/neo-daoism/. Accessed 11 March 2019.

Chen Guying. (2016). *The Philosophy of Life: A New Reading of the Zhuangzi*. New York: Brill.

Chau-kiu Cheung and Andrew Chi-fai Chan. (2005). "Philosophical Foundations of Eminent Hong Kong Chinese CEOs' Leadership." *Journal of Business Ethics* 60 (1): 47–62. Available online at https://doi.org/10.1007/s10551-005-2366-7. Accessed 18 June 2019.

Scott Cook. (1997). "Zhuang Zi and His Carving of the Confucian Ox." *Philosophy East and West* 47 (4): 521–53. Available online at https://doi.org/10.2307/1400301

C. Custer. (2016). "8 Lessons From Jack Ma's Favorite Book." *TechInAsia*, 16 September. Available online at www.techinasia.com/tk-lessons-jack-mas-favorite-book. Accessed 19 March 2019.

Financial Times. (2013). "Person of the Year: Jack Ma," 12 December.

Herbert Fingarette. (1972). *Confucius: The Secular as Sacred*. New York: Harper & Row.

Chad Hansen. (2017). "Daoism." In Edward N. Zalta (ed.), *Stanford Encyclopaedia of Philosophy*, Stanford, CA: Stanford University. (First published on 19 February 2003). Available online at https://plato.stanford.edu/archives/spr2017/entries/daoism/. Accessed 18 June 2019.

Hong Hai. (2007). "嵇康的养生思想与其文学创作" ["The Life Cultivation Principles of Ji Kang and Its Influence on His Literary Works"]. (Unpublished master's dissertation). Beijing: Beijing Normal University.

Hong Hai. (2016). *Principles of Chinese Medicine: A Modern Interpretation*, 2nd edition. London: Imperial College Press.

Craig Johnson. (2000). "Taoist Leadership Ethics." *Journal of Leadership and Organizational Studies* 7 (1): 82–91. Available online at https://doi.org/10.1177/107179190000700108. Accessed 18 July 2019.

Habibullah N. Karim. (2019). "Dysfunctional Superpowers on Both Sides of the Atlantic." *The Daily Star*, 22 January. Available online at www.thedailystar.net/opinion/global-affairs/news/dysfunctional-superpowers-both-sides-the-atlantic-1690855. Accessed 19 July 2019.

Mike Kilen. (2016). "Nov. 1, 1991: The Day a University Shooting Rampage Shocked Iowa." *Des Moines Register*, 28 October. Available online at www.desmoinesregister.

com/story/news/2016/10/28/nov-1-1991-day-university-shooting-rampage-shocked-iowa/92053548/. Accessed 18 July 2019.

Lao Tzu. (1963). *The Tao Te Ching*. Translated by D.C. Lau. London: Penguin Classics.

Lao Tzu. (1997). *Tao Te Ching*. Translated by Arthur Waley. Chatham: Wordsworth Classics.

G.E.R. Lloyd. (1990). *Demystifying Mentalities*. New York and Cambridge: Cambridge University Press.

G.E.R. Lloyd. (1991). *Methods and Problems in Greek Science: Selected Papers*. New York and Cambridge: Cambridge University Press.

Matthias Matthijs. (2016). "Dysfunctional Democracy and Referenda: The Case of Brexit." *World Politics Review*, 9 June. Available online at www.worldpoliticsreview.com/articles/19016/dysfunctional-democracy-and-referenda-the-case-of-brexit. Accessed 19 July 2019.

Julie E. Maybee. (2017). "Hegel's Dialectics." In Edward N. Zalta (ed.), *Stanford Encyclopaedia of Philosophy*. Stanford, CA: Stanford University. (First published on 3 June 2016). Available online at https://plato.stanford.edu/archives/win2016/entries/hegel-dialectics/. Accessed 19 July 2019.

Steven Lee Myers. (1991). "Student Opens Fire at U. of Iowa, Killing 4 Before Shooting Himself." *New York Times*, 2 November. Available online at www.nytimes.com/1991/11/02/us/student-opens-fire-at-u-of-iowa-killing-4-before-shooting-himself.html. Accessed 15 March 2019.

Christopher B. Nelson. (2015). "The Influential Book in Alibaba Founder Jack Ma's Briefcase." *Forbes*, 17 July. Available online at www.forbes.com/sites/christophernelson/2015/07/17/the-influential-book-in-alibaba-founder-jack-mas-briefcase/#22118295cf66. Accessed 19 March 2019.

Ni Peimin. (2010). "Kung Fu for Philosophers." *New York Times*, 8 December. Available online at https://opinionator.blogs.nytimes.com/2010/12/08/kung-fu-for-philosophers/. Accessed 19 July 2019.

Valrie Plaza. (2015). *American Mass Murderers*. USA: Lulu.com

Richard E. Nisbett (2003). *The Geography of Thought: How Asians and Westerners Think Differently . . . And Why*. New York: Free Press.

Richard E. Nisbett, Kaiping Peng, Incheol Choi and Ara Norenzayan. (2001). "Culture and Systems of Thought: Holistic Versus Analytic Cognition." *Psychological Review* 108 (2): 291–310. Available online at https://doi.org/10.1037/0033-295X.108.2.291. Accessed 18 July 2019.

İsmail Orhan Sönmez. (2015). "Tao of Management or The Way of Actionless Activity." *LinkedIn*, 19 November. Available online at www.linkedin.com/pulse/tao-management-way-actionless-activity-ismail-orhan-s%C3%B6nmez. Accessed 14 March 2019.

İsmail Orhan Sönmez. (2019). "Tao of the Management, The Way of Actionless Activity." *Doğru Yönetim: İnsan Yönetimi Yazıları*, 23 May. Available online at www.dogruyonetim.com/tum-yazilar/tao-of-the-management-the-way-of-actionless-activity/. Accessed 18 July 2019.

Francis Y.K. Soo. (1981). *Mao Tse-Tung Theory of Dialectic*. Dordrehct, Boston, MA and London: D. Reidel Publishing Company.

Julie Spencer-Rodgers, Helen C. Boucher, Sumi Mori, Lei Wang and Kaiping Peng. (2009). "The Dialectical Self-Concept: Contradiction, Change, and Holism in East Asian Cultures." *Personality and Social Psychology Bulletin* 35 (1): 29–44. Available online at https://doi.org/10.1177/0146167208325772. Accessed 19 July 2019.

Ning Su, Pratima Bansal and Pamela Laughland. (2017). "Alibaba Group: Technology, Strategy, and Sustainability." Case no. 9B16E036. London, Ontario: Richard Ivey School of Business Foundation. (Originally submitted on 12 June 2016).

Orville Schell. (2008). "China: Humiliation & the Olympics." New York Review of Books, 14 August. Reproduced in www.chinafile.com/library/nyrb-china-archive/china-humiliation-olympics. Accessed 15 March 2019.

Saori Tsukamoto, Elise Holland, Nick Haslam, Minoru Karasawa and Yoshihisa Kashima. (2014). "Cultural Differences in Perceived Coherence of the Self and Ingroup: A Japan – Australia Comparison." *Asian Journal of Social Psychology* 18 (1): 83–9. Available online at https://doi.org/10.1111/ajsp.12090. Accessed 18 June 2019.

Ludwig Wittgenstein. (2001) [1921]. *Tractatus Logico-Philosophicus*. Translated by D.F. Pears and B.F. McGuinness. London and New York: Routledge.

Julie M. Wulf. (2010). "Alibaba Group." Harvard Business School Case 710–436, March. (Revised April 2010).

Yang Mu Zhi. (1999). "Introductory Commentary on the English Translation of *Zhuangzi*." In Zhuangzi (ed.), *Zhuangzi*, Volumes 1 and 2. Translated into English by Wang Rongpei, and into modern Chinese by Qin Xuqing and Sun Yongchang, pp. 43–78. Changsha, China: Hunan People's Publishing House.

Yijun Xing and David Sims. (2011). "Leadership, Daoist Wu Wei and Reflexivity: Flow, Self-Protection and Excuse in Chinese Bank Managers' Leadership Practice." *Management Learning* 43 (1): 97–112. Available online at https://doi.org/10.1177/1350507611409659. Accessed 18 June 2019.

Alvin Ybanez. (2015). "Alibaba's Jack Ma Loves Magic, Philosophy, and Salt, Says Assistant." *Yibada*, 26 June. Available online at http://en.yibada.com/articles/41002/20150626/alibaba-jack-ma-loves-magic-philosophy-salt-assistant.htm. Accessed 19 March 2019.

Zhuangzi. (1999). *Zhuangzi*, Volumes 1 and 2. Translated into English by Wang Rongpei, and into modern Chinese by Qin Xuqing and Sun Yongchang. Changsha, China: Hunan People's Publishing House.

5

JAPANESE CULTURE AND MANAGEMENT

I believe that a company exists first and foremost to make its employees happy, and increasing sales and growing profits are nothing more than means of making employees happy.

(Tsukakoshi Hiroshi)[1]

Japan has been shaped by powerful internal and external forces ranging from the early introduction of Chinese agricultural technology and the importation of Confucianism and Buddhism, to the emergence of the samurai warrior ethos and the rise of nationalist imperialism leading to catastrophic defeat in World War II. The country's history helps to explain the effect of culture on corporate and state governance in an immensely complex society.

Japan's recorded history started much later than China's or Korea's. King Na of Wa sent emissaries to the Chinese court in AD 57,[2] but it was not until the Yamato period (circa AD 250–710) that regular contacts with China and Korea began.[3]

Ancient cultural history

Although Huntington's *Clash of Civilizations* classifies Japan in a separate category from China, the ancient culture of Japan drew deeply from the Chinese civilization.

Nara and Heian

The first powerful dynasty, the Yamato, founded near Nara, followed the Chinese centralized system of government, while their temples and palaces copied Chinese and Korean architectural designs.

The Japanese have always spoken their own language, but were without a writing system until they adopted the Chinese script called *kanji* (汉字). Chinese writing was used in education, official documents and public service communications. It was not until the ninth century AD that *kana*, the Japanese syllabary, was developed for use alongside *kanji*.[4]

During the important Nara period (710–794), the Japanese travelled a great deal to China and imported many daily implements and art artefacts. The capital was established in Nara, modelled after Chang'an, the Chinese Tang dynasty capital.

In the subsequent Heian period (794–1185), Emperor Kammu restored the Chinese *ritsuryo* (律令制度) system of centralized government and moved the capital to Heian-kyo (present-day Kyoto), where it remained the capital for the next thousand years. Contemporaneous with China's Tang and Song dynasties, Heian Japan actively acquired Buddhism, Confucianism, and other cultural resources from the Asian mainland. The period saw a flourishing of art and literature, and the publication of *The Tale of the Genji* (Figure 5.1), the world's first novel. Written by court lady Murasaki Shikibu, it captured, in vivid and meticulous detail, life in the imperial court with all its romance and intrigue.

Although the Imperial House of Japan nominally ruled the country, the real power was in the hands of an influential aristocratic family, the Fujiwara clan, which was allied to the imperial family through marriage, with many emperors having mothers from the clan.[5]

The mediaeval period (1185–1568) was a feudal era with powerful shoguns and warring states. The Taira emperor was overthrown in 1185 by warriors led by

FIGURE 5.1 Scene from *Tale of the Genji*[6]

Minamoto Yoritomo, who established the shogunate based in Eastern Japan. These four centuries of the feudal era spanned the Kamakura and Muromachi periods. It was an era dominated by warriors who also defended the country against the Mongol invasion in late thirteenth century. There was a brief restoration of imperial rule under Emperor Go-Daigo in 1333–1336, who was replaced by the Muromachi shogunate, with sporadic civil wars.

From around the mid-sixteenth century, which was the early modern period (1568–1868), we begin to see an attempted reunification of the country. During the Azuchi-Momoyama period (1568–1600), magnificent castles were built and unsuccessful attempts were made to suppress the growing power of samurais. The Shogun Tokugawa Ieyasu triumphed, and the capital moved to Edo city. The Edo period (1603–1867), also known as the Tokugawa era, began with the powerful Shogun Tokugawa Ieyasu based in Edo city while the court of the weakened emperor remained in Kyoto. It was, on the whole, a period of relative stability in Japan. Except for contact with the Dutch and Koreans, the country was quite secluded from the rest of the world.

One of the significant developments of the Edo era was the establishment of a centralized feudal structure, where the shogunate coexisted with the feudal lords. There were status distinctions between samurai, merchants, and peasants, but the samurai who wielded the sword were at the top of the power hierarchy.

By contrast, Chinese society since the Han dynasty had been ruled by the rich and powerful scholar-gentry class. The ruling Chinese mandarins sought to control and change society by influencing people's minds and enacting laws that would keep them disciplined in a Confucian moral society. The shoguns ruled with the sword. These cultural impulses may have something to do with Japan's later rise as an imperialistic world power. The Chinese, on the other hand, eschewed imperialism, but continued to strengthen their walls to defend against foreign invaders.

Tokugawa Ieyasu promoted Confucianism to Japanese society mainly for the purposes of enforcing social order and inculcating respect for authority. The Chinese "Four Books and Five Classics" became the core curriculum in schools during the late Tokugawa period. Tokugawa himself gave some acknowledgment to Confucian *ren*, urging benevolence even toward adversaries: "Requite malice with kindness." Confucianism became the most important source of moral precepts among the warrior class and commoners alike.

Shinto and Buddhism

As much as Daoism is native to China and Shamanism to Korea, Shinto derives from an animist form of religion in Japan that treats nature with spiritual respect. Ancient Japanese worshipped the sacred spirits they saw in rocks, mountains, rivers, and trees. The beautiful shrines that they erected to worship these deities became centres of cultural and daily living activities.

Today, most Japanese are not devotees of Shinto as a religion, but follow it as part of the traditional customs that emphasize purification and aesthetics in harmony with nature.[7] Others would visit Shinto shrines to honour ancestors and the spirits of other lives with whom they are connected. Some Japanese prime ministers traditionally visit the Yasukuni Shrine devoted to war dead from 1867–1951, much to the dismay of China and Korea who suffered from Japanese invasions before and during World War II.

Buddhism was first introduced to Japan around AD 552 from Paekche (sometimes Romanized as Baekje), one of the three rival kingdoms on the Korean peninsula.[8] Shinto-Buddhist syncretism evolved from there. Shinto shrines and their deities were combined with those of Buddhist temples. Many Japanese would visit Buddhist temples as well as pray for blessings at Shinto shrines.

Buddhism was deepened with further import from China during the Nara and Heian periods. The famous Hanshan (Cold Mountain) Temple (寒山寺) features three eminent monks in a hallowed hall, one of whom is Kong Hai (Kukai), a Japanese monk who studied Buddhism in China in the ninth century. He visited and stayed in Hanshan Temple to be tutored in Buddhism before returning to Japan where he started to preach Buddhism.[9] The Japanese continue to view Hanshan as one of the most notable temples in China. Thousands of Japanese visitors flock there each New Year's Eve to hear the temple's famous bell struck at midnight to herald in a new year.

Zen Buddhism is the Japanese version of Chan (禅) Buddhism in China that developed in the Tang and Song dynasties as a result of the percolation of Daoism into Buddhist thought. The essence of Zen is understanding life directly through meditation, without the intervention of logic or language. It became a separate school of Buddhism in the twelfth century during the Kamakura period (1185–1333), when Nonin established the first Zen school known as the Daruma school. In 1189, Nonin sent two students to China, and they secured recognition for Nonin as a Zen master.[10]

Zen appeared to fit the lifestyle of the samurai, confronting death without fear and acting largely by intuition.

The samurai tradition

The samurai (*bushi*) were the warriors of pre-modern Japan, who trace their origins to the Heian period campaigns to subdue the native Emishi people in the Tohoku region. The warriors were employed by wealthy landowners. They practised a warrior creed or *bushido* (the way of the warrior), and grew increasingly powerful. Samurais employed a formidable range of weapons, including bows and arrows, spears, and guns, but their main weapon was the *katana*, a long curved sword that could cut a man's body open with a single stroke.[11]

The samurais later evolved into a ruling military class and became the highest ranking social caste of the Edo period (1603–1867). *Bushido* stressed some Confucian values such as loyalty to one's master, self-discipline, and respect for hierarchy. Many samurais also practised Zen Buddhism.

Modern times: Western influences in the Japanese civilization

Around the period when China was reeling from the guns of Western "barbarians" in the Opium Wars, the shogunate at Edo was overcome by strong naval forces led by Commodore Perry, who forced the opening of Japanese ports through the Convention of Kanagawa in 1854. The imperial court overthrew the Shogunate and restored rule under the Emperor, culminating in the Meiji Restoration in 1868.

The Japanese capital, where the Emperor would hold court, was moved to Edo city, which was renamed Tokyo. The first restoration emperor, Meiji the Great, who donned Western attire, carried a sword and had the military bearing of a samurai, was a telling contrast to scholarly Chinese emperors like Qianlong (see Figures 5.2 and 5.3).

FIGURE 5.2 The Qianlong Emperor (1711–1799)[12]

FIGURE 5.3 Emperor Meiji the Great (1852–1912)[13]

In the Meiji period (1868–1912) the Emperor ruled over all of Japan, but yielded to the influence of Western power, trade, and technology. The role of the Emperor in the Meiji state was strengthened through the introduction of State Shinto ideology. Imperial scholars argued that Shinto reflected the divine origins of the Emperor, who ought to enjoy a privileged relationship with the Japanese state. The rites and rituals of Shinto were formulated with reverence to the Emperor. Together with Confucianism, Shinto provided the government with the "concepts and practices to formulate the principle for its nation-building efforts as a modern state as well as the spiritual bases to mobilize the populace."[14]

With the swing towards conservatism and nationalism in the late-Meiji period, social philosophers such as Inoue Tetsujiro advocated a return to national ethics based largely on selective Confucian virtues such as loyalty and filial piety. Confucian notions were elevated as an integral part of a "nationalistic, imperialistic, and militaristic blend serving the interests of Japanese militarists of the 1930s and 1940s."[15]

Westernization was advocated in an influential 1885 article "Datsu-A Ron" ("Goodbye Asia") by an anonymous author, thought to be influential writer and educator Fukuzawa Yukichi. He argued that Meiji Japan should abandon Qing China and Chosen Korea, and adopt modernity from the West whilst retaining the better aspects of Confucian values.[16]

Some of his writings amounted to a call for Japan to leave the Asian orbit and become part of the West:

> Once the wind of Western civilization blows to the East, every blade of grass and every tree in the East follow what the Western wind brings. . . . We do not have time to wait for the enlightenment of our neighbours so that we can work together toward the development of Asia. It is better for us to leave the ranks of Asian nations and cast our lot with civilized nations of the West. . . . We should deal with them exactly as the Westerners do.[17]

The rise of imperialism

As a result of Westernization, Japan rapidly rose to become an industrial and military power. Following in the footsteps of Western imperialistic powers like England and Spain was also consistent with the samurais' militant tradition.

Japan defeated the Chinese in battle in 1895, and the Russians in 1905. In 1900, Japan joined the infamous Eight-Nation Alliance formed to decimate the Chinese vigilantes of the Boxer Rebellion. It was the only Asian member and contributed the largest number of troops; the others were America and European powers. It was ironic that the Japanese, defeated by a Western invader at the beginning of the Meiji era, later joined Western powers to commit aggression in a neighbouring Asian country that had been the fount of much of its civilization.

Japan went on to annex Korea in 1910 and invade Manchuria in 1931, leading to full-scale war with China from 1937. She shocked the Americans in 1942 with the bombing of Pearl Harbour, and entered into the Pacific theatre of war in World War II.

Japan's spectacular post-war peacetime economic rise stalled after a severe blow from the 1985 Plaza Accord, under which Japan, the United States, and three European powers (France, Germany, and the United Kingdom) agreed to push the value of the US dollar down against the Japanese yen. Over two and a half years, up to early 1988, the yen *doubled* in value against the dollar. By the early 1990s, the nation plunged into recession then stagnation from which she has yet to recover. Although other factors like an ageing demographic and the rise of East Asian tiger economies like China and South Korea contributed to Japanese decline, there is speculation that the Americans were "desperate to stymie Japan's economic rise"[18] so as to prevent the nation's fulfilment of Ezra Vogel's prediction of "Japan as No. 1."[19]

Japan's twentieth-century ambition to be an imperialistic world power alongside the West was thwarted by Europe and America in World War II; her economy was also damaged in the late twentieth century by the Plaza Accord. Yet today, she aligns herself with the Western powers, enjoying almost the status of an honorary Western nation when its roots are deeply Asian Buddhist and Confucian. One cannot help but speculate that uneasy internal conflicts rage deep in the Japanese psyche beneath its calm decorous exterior.

Confucianism in contemporary society

In contemporary Japanese society, the remnant influence of Confucianism is only one of a number of competing ideologies and cultural identities in Japanese thought. It is pervasive in the workplace, where employers typically show Confucian benevolence to employees. Although there have been changes, women are often accorded lower status in the workplace, a relic from traditional Confucian attitudes towards the primary role of women in the home.

Certain practices associated with the influence of Confucianism persist, for example reverence for ancestors expressed through ancestor worship. Smith provides illuminating accounts of the reactions of three Japanese persons to the question of whether they had Confucian values. The first reported that she knew little about Confucianism, but, after reading about it from a book, discovered that Confucian thought had quietly filtered into "fundamental ways of thinking" in her life, possibly through education. The second admitted to being taught to respect older people and superiors, but did not realize that was Confucian. The third, a Japanese college teacher in Honolulu, said he was more impressed with Korean students who "work hard, are humble, and carry around a lot of Confucian values that are absent in the new breed of Japanese."[20]

Confucian temples can be found in many parts of Japan. Some of them engage in colourful festivals to pray to Confucius as a deity, with *gagaku* (ancient court dances and music) and offerings such as rice cakes, pheasant meat, and sake to the statue of Confucius and his disciples like Yanzi and Mencius.[21]

But it is in the hard-driving competitive world of business corporations that Confucianism may be found in its subtle but enduring influence, as we shall see in the rest of this chapter.

Culture and the Japanese firm

Unlike in China where it has set the standards for social and political order for over two millennia, Confucianism in Japan reached a high point of influence during the Tokugawa era. During those two and a half centuries, it was practised as a form of social utilitarianism that evolved into an ethical code. Less forgiving commentators regarded it as a source of authoritarianism "at its most repressive stage."[22]

After Japan's violent encounter with the West ushered in the Meiji period, Confucian influence in the country ebbed. However, Confucian ideology had already permeated deeply into Japanese culture. Although Confucian texts were not widely used in schools, some of the outstanding corporate leaders of the Meiji era were steeped in Confucian ideals. One of them was Shibusawa Eiichi (1840–1931), known as the "father of Japanese capitalism." He founded numerous corporations, sat on many boards, and was president of the First National Bank of Japan. He was active in philanthropy, supporting hospitals, schools, and social service programmes. Shibusawa saw Confucian ethics as an integral part of economic life and placed the pursuit of the public interest before the accumulation of private wealth. Morality for him was the *Analects* of Confucius and the economy the abacus, an idea that he propounded with the enigmatic dictum, "The *Analects* and the abacus are inseparable."[23] Shibusawa's brand of Confucian capitalism sought to create both ethical guidelines and a moral identity for business leaders. It has contributed to the distinctiveness of Japanese versus Western corporate philosophy. As Shibusawa's biographer and critic John Sagers puts it:

> Shibusawa called himself a business leader or "person of practical affairs" *jitsugyoka*. Where government and military officials defended the nation and carried out policies, *jitsugyoka* produced valuable goods and services that contributed to the people's well-being. . . . Unlike Tokugawa-era merchants who were greedy for gain for their households, *jitsugyoka* worked for the good of the whole nation. Furthermore, his Confucianism allowed him to define himself in contrast to foreign and domestic liberals who called for Japan's wholesale Westernization.[24]

Confucian ethics is most obvious in the concept of the *entity* firm, which contrasts with the shareholder wealth-maximizing firm in Western capitalism.

The entity firm versus the property firm

The modern firm in the West has traditionally been held to belong exclusively to shareholders. Until recently, business school students were taught the crass notion that the role of the management of a corporation was to maximize the wealth of the corporation's shareholders. Social pressure has over recent decades driven corporations to place some attention on corporate social responsibility (CSR). But even today, stripped of pretensions of social objectives and love for its employees, the firm is still basically seen as belonging to shareholders. The job of the board of directors is to be custodians of this ownership. Their long-term actions are aimed at ensuring the financial welfare of the owners, while demonstrating politically correct respect for the environment, enlightened human resource policies, and a trusted benign image to its customers – all these help to attain long-term profitability.

But even as late as the early twenty-first century, legal experts at Harvard pronounced that the "end of history" had arrived. Consensus had been reached over the role and responsibility of corporate management. It was announced that

> managers of the corporation should be charged with the obligation to manage the corporation in the interests of its shareholders; that other corporate constituencies, such as creditors, employees, suppliers, and customers should

have their interests protected by contractual and regulatory means rather than through participation in corporate governance; and that the principal measure of the interests of the publicly traded corporations' shareholders is the market value of their shares in the firm.[25]

Ironically, this pronouncement was followed in quick succession by the collapse of several large shareholder wealth-maximizing companies, including Enron, Arthur Andersen, and WorldCom. In 2008, the demise of Lehman Brothers under the weight of adventurous profit-maximizing greed exacerbated the global financial crisis. These failures prompted Jack Welch of General Electric, respected doyen of American corporate chieftains, to declare that pursuing shareholder value as a strategy was "the dumbest idea ever."[26]

In Japan, the business firm has traditionally not been viewed in the unequivocal hard-nosed way of the West. Rather, the firm is an *entity* in society that provides good employment, serves customers, and contributes to social development and the quality of the environment. It is cooperative with the government, whose role is to maintain political stability and business infrastructure to allow the management of the corporation to run it effectively for the benefit of these various constituencies of the firm, including its shareholders.

Citing a distinction made by *The Financial Times* between "property" firms and "entity" firms, Dore characterized the classical profit-maximizing Western firm as the former, in the sense that it is treated as the property of the shareholders, reflecting the ideology of "shareholder capitalism." The traditional Japanese firm as an entity has a personality and mission all of its own, not wholly or even mainly determined by its shareholders. To borrow Dore's homely analogy, the entity firm is "like a school, university or public institution which continues through time and has a reputation of its own, irrespective of the people who are, at any one time, working in it."[27]

As an entity firm is not dominated by the profit objectives of the firm's shareholders, there is a prudent and sensitive balancing of the needs and expectations of its various constituencies. This reality was not lost on me in my past corporate career during dealings with a Japanese distributor for our company's products. The young and soft-spoken company president had only taken over the helm of this privately owned company (a household name in Japan) from his father a few years earlier. Intellectually inclined and keen on innovation, he had introduced some radical changes which soaked up much of the company's savings through making new investments. The directors of the company, most of whom had been appointed during the tenure of his late father, were alarmed and decided to intervene, removing him from the office and relegating him to a corporate planning role with no executive power. Even though he and his mother held a controlling stake in the company, they were powerless to remove those directors for two years. That gave the directors sufficient time to roll back some of the changes and put the company on a more conservative footing, thereby offering reassurance of security to the company's other stakeholders.

Virtues of the Japanese entity firm

One of the distinguishing features of the Japanese entity firm is lifetime employment, with employees typically regarding the company as their second home to which they devote a lifetime of loyalty and dedication. In return, they are nurtured, rewarded, and taken care of for life.

Related to lifetime employment is the Confucian-inspired regard for seniority based largely on age and years of service to the firm. Promotion would be based on seniority as well as performance. This does not prevent rivalry for top corporate positions like those of managing directors and president. But even for such positions, one's personal influence in the company's internal community, and ability to cooperate with others and gain their respect, would play a significant role in promotions.

The government plays a key supporting role in corporate Japan. As Vogel has observed, there has been a close nexus between the bureaucrats of the civil service and the top echelons of corporate Japan.[28] This continues even to the present day.[29] Typically, graduates recruited from elite universities like Tokyo, Waseda, and Keio would advance together in the organization for the first half of their careers. At one point, after a number of them make it to the top posts, many of the others would be recruited into senior positions in large conglomerates like Mitsui and Sumitomo, where they are likely to find one or two of their former bosses already in key positions. These relationships are integral to corporate Japan, as they help to keep the objectives of the country's key industries alive and promote ideals that go beyond shareholder welfare.

Industrial strikes are rare in Japan as a result of the trust and mutual regard that employees and management have for each other as well as the commonality of interest. This is reflected in "enterprise-based unions" derived from the communitarian philosophy that employees and management are in the same boat and share a long-term common destiny. In traditional Western societies, labour and capital as factors of production owned by different sets of people are clearly delineated. Many of the disputes in Western industrial economies involve bargaining over the returns enjoyed by capital versus those by labour. In a Japanese enterprise-based union, there is an understanding that these returns do not constitute a zero-sum game. Employees are aware that they are the trustees of the enterprise's future. They work together to fulfil the common objectives of keeping the company going and thriving. One result of this corporate ideology is that the difference between the wages of colleagues in the same age group can be as low as 20 percent.[30]

The cultural ideology of thinking in the long term extends to Japanese firms' relationships with their customers and suppliers. It can take decades for a brand name to establish itself in the daily lives of its customers. Often, the brand is handed down from one generation to another, and its reputation for quality and reliability is treasured and protected by the company's employees who view themselves as its custodians.

The same philosophy extends to suppliers. Each supplier is scrupulously researched and tested for a long-term relationship, and changes can be made only with great difficulty and trauma to both supplier and the purchasing firm. This kind of relational trading, akin to *guanxi*, is based on knowledge, trust, and an established track record of the supplier. Foreigners new to business with the Japanese often regard this as a kind of protectionism, because they may not be sensitive to such requirements of Japanese firms and find the fulfilment of conditions to qualify as a supplier vexing and prohibitively difficult.

I recall a friend who set up a factory in the city of Yangzhou in Jiangsu province, China, to export dumplings and finger foods to restaurants in Japan serving Chinese food. It took the factory several gruelling years to gain acceptance following many visits by Japanese experts and submissions of factory layout and procedures, cleanliness protocols, and the hygiene habits of its workers. After the factory won approval, it became only one of two in China to gain acceptance, and has since enjoyed a profitable and satisfying business.

The changing face of corporate Japan

Many small- to medium-sized Japanese corporations retain key aspects of the entity firm. Larger publicly listed companies face new pressures with many shareholders, including foreign institutional investors who may have different expectations from the traditional companies.

Ina: the quintessential entity firm

Ina Food Industry is a medium-sized company that manufactures powdered agar and gelatine products, having seen profit growth for most of half a century. Much of its success in recent years may be credited to its long-serving CEO Tsukakoshi Hiroshi, whose humble beginnings taught him the virtue of good health and hard work.[31]

Ina's motto, "Let us build a good company," reflects its family as well as the communitarian values of its employees. Tsukakoshi studiously eschewed Western management indicators of growth and profit for company performance, concentrating instead on the longevity of the company's role to serve customers through research to continually improve its products, and by placing employee happiness and welfare as top priority.

As chief executive of Ina, Tsukakoshi struck a fine balance between the scale of the company and its obligations to employees, suppliers, customers, and to society through patronage of the arts. The company's physical environment is relaxing yet invigorating, with landscaped gardens and facilities one would find in private homes.

Tsukakoshi applied himself rigorously as a promoter of egalitarian growth (employees benefit equally) and as an arbitrator between various stakeholders' interests. He perpetually tried to be helpful to society. During the 2005 demand boom, Tsukakoshi boosted production capacity to cater to consumers who appealed to him for more supply as they appreciated the health benefits of Ina's products. This was achieved at a lower profit and greater stress to his employees who had to work longer hours. The company also insisted on the healthy, natural way of producing agar with seaweed, instead of chemicals which would yield better profit.

When a proposal was offered to take the company public through an initial public offering (IPO), Tsukakoshi turned it down as he felt an infusion of numerous public shareholders would compromise their corporate culture and mission. The company refused to step up exports even in the face of strong overseas demand, again because it felt that increased production to satisfy overseas customers would injure the company's corporate culture in the long run.

After retirement, Tsukakoshi became a management guru of sorts, spreading his philosophy of the "tree-ring growth model," which prescribes slow but steady growth like the number of rings on a big tree that increases each year. His company welcomes a steady stream of visiting executives and analysts from major corporations, including Murata Manufacturing and the Toyota Group.[32]

Companies like Ina are certainly not uncommon in contemporary Japan. The charismatic chairman Matsumoto Akira of the public listed Calbee Inc. food group speaks openly against shareholder capitalism, placing stock owners only fourth in priority after customers, employees, and community. He argues that only by ignoring them and focussing instead on the greater good of the company can he eventually serve their needs. "It's shareholders last," he said in an interview in Tokyo, "That's actually the best thing for them."[33]

The Toyota way and the challenge of new times

The Toyota Motor Corporation is the largest automobile producer in the world and one of Japan's most admired companies. Its company culture and employee credo have often been held up as a model for other corporations in the country.

The Toyota people culture is shared by the best of Japanese companies. It incorporates a consensus management style, respect for hierarchy, and communitarian values emphasizing the interest of the group over that of the individual.[34] The company provides continuous training and re-education to keep employees up-to-date with technology and enable them to acquire new skills.

The Confucian respect for authority and hierarchy allows for firmness in decision-making. Decisions are not always made at great speed, as there is a consensus-seeking process in which ideas flow from below and are considered and debated before higher management makes the final call. Once the final decision is made, it is quickly implemented without further contention.

However, the company's success and Japan's opening up of its economy to foreign investment has attracted foreign institutions. Changes in the Japanese corporate scene over the last ten years may be gradually forcing its transformation to a more shareholder-oriented company.

Economic stagnation in Japan from the 1990s and the insidious penetration of American business values have taken a toll on the culture of some of Japan's largest companies. Deregulation and the banking crisis of 1997 led to a decline of crossholdings of shares by major groups, opening the way for the influence of independent shareholders in search of returns on investment. This included foreign investors, in particular, American institutional investors who wield great power at shareholder meetings open to the public.

An increasing number of MBAs trained in American graduate schools began to occupy key positions in traditional companies, exerting pressure on reforming compensation policies so that they are determined more by performance than by seniority. Corporate ethics and governance began a worrying decline even as loyalty to employers remained resilient, prompting the quip by economist Hugh Patrick that, in America, employees steal from the firm, but in Japan employees steal *for* the firm.[35]

The mighty Toyota was not spared these changes. Flaws in its armour surfaced and turned into tragic cracks. The vaunted Toyota Way rewards intense company loyalty to the point of suppressing challenges to authority and, at times, even discouraging constructive criticism aimed at doing things better. This is a culture of control, as argued by Saruta Masaki.[36] The result was that the leadership of the company descended into managerial dissonance when a crisis broke out on foreign soil. The *Wall Street Journal* gleefully labelled Toyota's botched handling of the sticky gas pedal problem in 2010 "A Crisis Made in Japan."[37]

Corporate scandals: Olympus and Toshiba

Two years later, a different crisis erupted at the respected optical products company Olympus. It grew into a full-blown scandal involving fraud committed by its board of directors, which had knowingly over-reported profits to its shareholders on the Tokyo Stock Exchange. The conspiracy of silence was divulged by whistle-blower Michael Woodford, an Englishman who had earlier been promoted to president after a long career in the company's European operations.[38]

When the scandal broke, the Western press displayed little tolerance for such naked breach of corporate governance and made an international hero of Woodford, who was dismissed from the company. Olympus apologized publicly and rectified its accounts. The reaction from the Japanese public was more ambivalent, suggesting that such transgressions of corporate governance were viewed with more equanimity by local people in the know, who regarded these offences as having few victims, as they knew how to look at other indications of company performance beyond reported earnings.

The main discrepancy in the company's published accounts arose from concealing losses from bad investments. Having admitted to fraud, the company maintained that it had no major impact on business. The statement would also have implied that investors in Olympus stock would as a whole have suffered little net loss – those who bought shares based on inflated profit suffered a wealth transfer to those who had sold the shares to them at inflated prices.

Among the Japanese, sympathy for Woodford was ambiguous. From the point of view of Japanese culture, he had committed the ultimate sin of disloyalty to the company, shamed its leadership, and damaged its public image. It also harmed the standing of corporate Japan in international circles.

Could Woodford have persuaded the board to quietly write back these losses and amortize them over a period of time so that its impact on the company's bottom line would be less traumatic? Did he have a personal grievance or a hidden agenda to harm the company, and was he aspiring to be anointed a hero in the final years of his business career? Or was he merely respectful of international standards of corporate governance and prepared to put his career on the line for the sake of being faithful to his principles?

To some conservative Japanese corporate leaders, the Englishman was a bull in a Japanese shop. He did not understand that Olympus accounts would eventually have been self-correcting once the discrepancies were quietly rectified. Instead, he plunged the company into a crisis that destroyed value for shareholders, customers, and suppliers.

Before Olympus finally admitted to the deception, Japan's mainstream media and regulators kept a discreet silence. Even after the fact, Japanese institutional shareholders did not voice any noticeable criticism.[39] Only Prime Minister Noda made the perfunctory comment, directed possibly at the ears of global investors, that capitalism worked the same way in Japan as elsewhere in the world.

For traditional corporate leaders of Japan, there were few winners from the foreign manager's dramatic disclosures. But they could not possibly have denied that it was a valuable lesson for corporate Japan, which had to move with the times. An increasing number of younger managers were more comfortable with Western-style governance, and large foreign shareholders expected transparency and information integrity for them to make informed investment decisions.

The lesson was made more painful by the fact that, once again, as happened with Commodore Perry and the bomb dropped on Hiroshima, it was the West (in the person of Woodford) that inflicted the humiliating punishment.

A similar scandal broke out a few years later at another icon of Japanese technology, manufacturing giant Toshiba Corporation. The company's real profitability had been flagging and pressure to show a profit led to top management doctoring the books over the past seven years.[40] The magnitude of the deception was larger than Olympus' but, thanks to the country's recent experience dealing with such scandals, it was handled swiftly with an external investigation committee set up by the Securities and Exchange Commission. The four-member committee looked at accounts from 2009 to 2014, and found a series of accounting entries that showed an overstatement of ¥152 billion (US$1.2 billion) in net profit. Toshiba President Tanaka Hisao and his predecessors Nishida Atsutoshi and Sasaki Norio were involved in the manipulation, and there were no internal systems in place to stop them.

The Nissan saga and Japan's culture of the entity firm

The sacking of the boss of giant automaker Nissan in November 2018 was the climax of a Japanese corporate saga that sent shockwaves through the international business community. It had all the appearance of a scandal driven by poor corporate governance. More likely, it also reflected the deeply embedded traditional culture of corporate Japan.

Carlos Ghosn, a Brazilian-born French executive, was arrested on suspicion of financial misconduct and dismissed from his post as chairman of the Japanese car giant Nissan.[41] His arrest scuttled prospects for a global corporate alliance that would effectively merge Renault, Nissan, and Mitsubishi. A loose alliance through cross-shareholdings had already been formed in 1999, when Renault rescued Nissan from bankruptcy by taking a 43 percent stake in Nissan, while Nissan had a 15 percent stake in Renault. In 2016, Mitsubishi was added after it was found to be struggling financially.

Although the three companies act as a global car grouping, each retains its distinct identity while sharing common technologies and parts suppliers. Carlos Ghosn had been chairman of Nissan and Mitsubishi as well as chairman and chief executive of Renault. He had bigger plans to bring the three component firms together in what was tantamount to a merger. This raised alarm bells at Nissan, which neither wanted to lose its identity nor come under the control of the French Renault as majority shareholder.

The Japanese management at Nissan appeared to have participated in the move to foil Ghosn's plans. They might have acted to block a merger that threatened the identity of Nissan as a Japanese entity firm whose stakeholders were Japanese staff, management, shareholders, suppliers, and customers. If that was the case, it would have been an act of loyalty to preserve a Japanese icon.

Conclusion

The scandals of Toyota, Olympus, Toshiba, and Nissan reveal that the rise of international shareholders as players in the management of large Japanese companies is fraught with complexity and internal tensions, especially considering that the notion of the entity firm remains deep in Japanese culture. The onslaught of shareholder wealth-maximizing Western capitalism, fronted by international investors and Japanese executives with MBAs minted in America and Europe, will play out for a long time to come. It will be a severe test for corporate Japan's Confucian roots. Companies like Ina catering mainly to the domestic market may well preserve their traditional corporate values, but globalization and international competition will pressure the large conglomerate *keiretsus* to restructure their corporate governance and management priorities to be in line with Western emphasis on shareholder wealth.

Amidst this turmoil, there has been a revival of the Confucian philosophical vision of Shibusawa Eiichi who placed morality and the public interest above profit maximization. In the wake of the 2008 financial meltdown, faith in capitalism has waned and there have been louder calls for "the taming, if not outright abolition, of capitalism."[42] A new ¥10,000 banknote has been planned for issue in 2024, as if to remind the Japanese business world of the ideals that had driven their great corporations since the Meiji era.[43]

Ironically, if China were to dominate Asia as an economic and military super-power, Japan's preservation of her corporate cultural heritage may well lie in a political realignment of the country with Asia. It would be a reversal of Meiji *Datsu-A Ron* and a return to the country's traditional origins. It is a prospect too tenuous and distant to contemplate, but perhaps not to be totally dismissed.

Notes

1 Tsukakoshi (2015). See also Anderson's (2015) brief review of it.
2 National Museum of Japanese History. (n.d.).
3 *Kodansha Encyclopedia of Japan* (1999), p. 810.
4 See "Classical Japan: Japanese Use of Chinese Writing System," on Columbia University's Asian Topics website at http://afe.easia.columbia.edu/at/cl_japan/cj09.html.
5 F.W. Seal. (n.d.).
6 Picture from https://upload.wikimedia.org/wikipedia/commons/7/79/Kiritsubo_LACMA_M.2007.152.37.jpg.
7 Tamashige (2013).
8 National Museum of Japanese History. (n.d.).
9 Travel China Guide. (n.d.). "Hanshan Temple (Cold Mountain Temple)." Available online at www.travelchinaguide.com/attraction/jiangsu/suzhou/hanshan_temple.htm. Accessed 24 April 2019.
10 Dumoulin (2005), pp. 7–8.
11 Japan-guide.com. (n.d.). "Samurai." Available online at www.japan-guide.com/e/e2127.html. Accessed 24 April 2019.
12 Picture from https://commons.wikimedia.org/wiki/File:Qianlong-alt2.jpg.
13 Picture from https://commons.wikimedia.org/wiki/File:The_Americana_-_a_universal_reference_library,_comprising_the_arts_and_sciences,_literature,_history,_biography,_geography,_commerce,_etc._of_the_world_(1903)_(14761612426).jpg.
14 Shimazono (2005), p. 12. See also Kwok (2009).
15 Tucker (2018).
16 Fukuzawa (1960) [1885], pp. 238–40, referenced in Kwok (2009), p. 32l; and in Tanaka (1995), p. 115.
17 Fukuzawa (1885). "Datsu-A Ron," *Jiji Shimpo*, 16 March 1885. Reprinted in Fukuzawa (1960) [1885], pp. 238–40. This English translation is cited in "Fukuzawa Yukichi," Wikiquote, part of Wikipedia: The Free Encyclopedia. Available online at https://en.wikiquote.org/wiki/Fukuzawa_Yukichi. Accessed 15 May 2019.
18 Yeung (2019).
19 Vogel (1979).
20 Smith (1996), pp. 172–3.
21 See Kyushu Tourism Promotion Organization's (2019) article on the Taku Confucian Temple Sekisai Festival at www.welcomekyushu.com/event/?mode=detail&id=9999900056420&isSpot=&isEvent=1. Accessed 6 July 2019.
22 Smith (1996), p. 159.
23 Tanaka (2017).
24 Sagers (2018), pp. 113–14. See also Morgan's (2019) review of Sagers' (2018) book.
25 Hansmann and Kraakman (2000).
26 Schumpeter blog (2015a) and Schumpeter blog (2015b).
27 Dore (2004).
28 Vogel (1979).
29 Fukada (2010).
30 Dore (2004), p. 1.
31 Information on Ina is derived principally from Misawa's (2006) study for the Asia Case Research Centre (ACRC).

32 His thoughts are compiled in the book *Tree-Ring Management*, published by the Japan Publishing Industry Foundation for Culture in 2015.
33 Redmond and Taniguchi (2018).
34 Treece (2006).
35 Dore (2008), p. 373.
36 Saruta Masaki is the author of several books on Toyota. His remarks on this aspect of Toyota's culture were cited in Glionna (2010): "The real Toyota Way is a culture of control. The company is very proud of this concept. They've been doing it for 50 years."
37 Kingston (2010).
38 Whipp and Soble (2011); Bloomberg (2012).
39 K.N.C. (2012).
40 Nagata (2015).
41 Leggett and Palumbo (2018).
42 See Morgan (2019), pp. 91–9, in which he reviews Sagers (2018).
43 Unseen Japan (2019).

References

Katie Anderson. (2015). "'Tree Ring Management': Take the Long View." Blog post, 30 October. Available online at https://kbjanderson.com/tree-ring-management-take-the-long-view/. Accessed 15 May 2019.

Bloomberg. (2012). "Olympus' ¥32 Billion Loss Tops Estimates." *Japan Times*, 2 February. Available online at www.japantimes.co.jp/news/2012/02/14/business/olympus-32-billion-loss-tops-estimates/#.XTSkknsRXIU. Accessed 22 July 2019.

Columbia University. (n.d.). "Classical Japan: Japanese Use of Chinese Writing System." *Asian Topics: An Online Resource for Asian History and Culture*. Available online at http://afe.easia.columbia.edu/at/cl_japan/cj09.html. Accessed 24 April 2019.

Ronald Dore. (2004). *Japanese-Style Management: Has it survived? Will it survive?* Tokyo: Research Institute of Economy, Trade and Industry (RIETI), 8 September.

Ronald Dore. (2008). "Insider Management and Board Reform: For Whose Benefit?" In Masahiko Aoki, Gregory Jackson and Hideaki Miyajima (eds.), *Corporate Governance in Japan: Institutional Change and Organizational Diversity*, 370–98. Oxford: Oxford University Press.

Heinrich Dumoulin. (2005). *Zen Buddhism: A History. Volume 2: Japan*. Translated by James W. Heisig and Paul Knitter. Indiana: World Wisdom Books.

Takahiro Fukada. (2010). "Looking Back at 'Japan as No. 1'." *Japan Times*, 11 November. Available online at www.japantimes.co.jp/news/2010/11/11/national/looking-back-at-japan-as-no-1/#.XTSqxHsRXIV. Accessed 4 April 2019.

Fukuzawa Yukichi. (1960). "Datsu-A Ron." In Fukuzawa Yukichi (ed.), *Fukuzawa Yukichi zenshu, dai 10 kan*. Tokyo: Iwanami shoten. (Original work published as an anonymous editorial in *Jiji Shimpo* on 16 March 1885).

John M. Glionna. (2010). "Toyota's Rigid Culture Criticized in Light of Recalls – Automaker's Toyota Way Handbook Dictates Details of Employees' Lives, Even in their Off Time." *Chicago Tribune*, 24 March. Available online at www.chicagotribune.com/news/ct-xpm-2010-03-24-sc-biz-0325-toyota-man-20100324-story.html. Accessed 22 July 2019.

Henry Hansmann and Reinier Kraakman. (2000). "The End of History for Corporate Law." Harvard Law School, Discussion Paper no. 280 3/2000. Available online at www.law.harvard.edu/programs/olin_center/papers/pdf/280.pdf. Accessed 4 April 2019.

Jeff Kingston. (2010). "A Crisis Made in Japan." *Wall Street Journal*, 5 February. Available online at www.wsj.com/articles/SB10001424052748704533204575047370633234414. Accessed 22 July 2019.

K.N.C. (2012). "The Olympus Scandal: Sayonara to All that." *The Economist*, 7 January. Available online at www.economist.com/schumpeter/2012/01/07/sayonara-to-all-that. Accessed 22 July 2019.

Kodansha Encyclopedia of Japan. (1999). "Japan: Chronology of Japanese History." Tokyo: Kodansha.

Dwight Tat Wai Kwok. (2009). "A Translation of Datsu-A Ron: Decoding a Prewar Japanese Nationalistic Theory." (Unpublished master's dissertation). Toronto, Canada: University of Toronto.

Kyushu Tourism Promotion Organization. (2019). "Taku Confucian Temple Sekisai Festival." Available online at www.welcomekyushu.com/event/?mode=detail&id=9999900056420&isSpot=&isEvent=1. Accessed 6 July 2019.

Theo Leggett and Daniele Palumbo (2018). "Carlos Ghosn: Five Charts on the Nissan Boss Scandal." *BBC News*, 25 November. Available online at www.bbc.com/news/business-46321097. Accessed 14 May 2019.

Mitsuru Misawa. (2006). *Ina Food Industry: A New Management Philosophy for Japanese Businesses.* A case study for the Asia Case Research Centre (ACRC), University of Hong Kong, Ref. 06/205C, November. Cambridge, MA: Harvard Business Review Press.

Jason Morgan. (2019). "Book Review of *Confucian Capitalism: Shibusawa Eiichi, Business Ethics, and Economic Development in Meiji Japan.*" *Quarterly Journal of Austrian Economics* 22 (1): 91–9. Available online at https://mises.org/library/confucian-capitalism-shibusawa-eiichi-business-ethics-and-economic-development-meiji-japan. Accessed 22 July 2019.

Kazuaki Nagata. (2015). "Pressure to Show a Profit Led to Toshiba's Accounting Scandal." *Japan Times*, 18 September. Available online at www.japantimes.co.jp/news/2015/09/18/business/corporate-business/pressure-to-show-a-profit-led-to-toshibas-accounting-scandal/#.XNuOhVIzbX. Accessed 15 May 2019.

National Museum of Japanese History. (n.d.). "Japanese Chronological Table." Available online at www.rekihaku.ac.jp

Tom Redmond and Takako Taniguchi. (2018). "Japan's Star Businessman Who Ignores His Investors to Make them Rich." *Japan Times*, 27 August. Available online at www.japantimes.co.jp/news/2018/08/27/business/corporate-business/japans-star-businessman-ignores-investors-make-rich/#.XTSplnsRXIU. Accessed 18 June 2019.

John H. Sagers (2018). *The Confucian Capitalism: Shibusawa Eiichi, Business Ethics, and Economic Development in Meiji Japan.* Cham, Switzerland: Palgrave Macmillan.

Schumpeter blog. (2015a). "The Business of Business: An Old Debate About What Companies are for Has Been Revived." *The Economist*, 19 March. Available online at www.economist.com/business/2015/03/19/the-business-of-business. Accessed 22 July 2019.

Schumpeter blog. (2015b). "Firm Beliefs: 'Asian' Corporate Values Seem to be Making a Comeback – But Appearances Are Deceptive." *The Economist*, 26 March. Available online at www.economist.com/business/2015/03/26/firm-beliefs. Accessed 22 July 2019.

F.W. Seal. (n.d.). "Heian Period: Court and Clan." Available online at www.samurai-archives.com/HeianPeriod.html. Accessed 24 April 2019.

Susumu Shimazono. (2005). "State Shinto and the Religious Structure of Modern Japan." *Journal of the American Academy of Religion* 73 (4): 1077–98. Available online at www.jstor.org/stable/4139766. Accessed 22 July 2019.

Robert J. Smith. (1996). "The Japanese (Confucian) Family." In Tu Wei-ming (ed.), *Confucian Traditions in East Asian Modernity: Moral Education and Economic Culture in Japan and the Four Mini-dragons*, 155–74. Cambridge, MA: Harvard University Press.

Sachiko Tamashige. (2013). "Seeing Where Shinto and Buddhism Cross." *Japan Times*, 16 May 2013. Available online at www.japantimes.co.jp/culture/2013/05/16/arts/seeing-where-shinto-and-buddhism-cross/#.XTS6UnsRXIV. Accessed 24 April 2019.

Tanaka Kazuhiro. (2017). "The 'Analects' and the Abacus: The Contemporary Relevance of Shibusawa Eiichi's Business Philosophy." *Nippon.com*, 5 January. Available online at www.nippon.com/en/currents/d00274/the-analects-and-the-abacus-the-contemporary-relevance-of-shibusawa-eiichi%E2%80%99s-business-ph.html. Accessed 5 July 2019.

Stefan Tanaka. (1995). *Japan's Orient: Rendering Pasts into History*. Berkeley, Los Angeles, CA and London: University of California Press.

James B. Treece. (2006). "The Roots of Toyota's Strength: The Japanese Powerhouse Manages the Complexities of Manufacturing Relentlessly." *Automotive News*, 14 August. Available online at www.autonews.com/article/20060814/SUB/60809022/the-roots-of-toyota-s-strength. Accessed 22 July 2019.

Tsukakoshi Hiroshi. (2015). *Tree-Ring Management: Take the Long View and Grow Your Business Slowly*. Translated by Hart Larrabee. Tokyo: Japan Publishing Industry Foundation for Culture.

John Tucker. (2018). "Japanese Confucian Philosophy." In Edward N. Zalta (ed.), *Stanford Encyclopedia of Philosophy*. Stanford, CA: Stanford University. (First published on 20 May 2008). Available online at https://plato.stanford.edu/archives/spr2018/entries/japanese-confucian/. Accessed 15 May 2019.

Unseen Japan. (2019). "Revolutionary Faces of Japan's New Currency." *medium.com*, 9 May. Available online at https://medium.com/@unseenjapan/the-revolutionary-faces-of-japans-new-currency-6707dbaaef47. Accessed 5 July 2019.

Ezra Vogel. (1979). *Japan as Number One: Lessons for America*. Cambridge, MA: Harvard University Press.

Lindsay Whipp and Jonathan Soble. (2011). "Olympus Management 'Rotten at the Core'." *Financial Times*, 7 December. Available online at www.ft.com/content/c61a2bd0-1fb2-11e1-9916-00144feabdc0. Accessed 22 July 2019.

Karen Yeung. (2019). "China Urged to Avoid Cautionary Tale of Japan and the Plaza Accord in Currency Deal with US." *South China Morning Post*, 26 February. Available online at www.scmp.com/economy/china-economy/article/2187773/china-urged-avoid-cautionary-tale-japan-and-plaza-accord. Accessed 22 July 2019.

6

CULTURE AND CHANGING GOVERNANCE IN KOREA

The more an unethically behaving [Korean] CEO gets shamed, the more the public is prepared to forgive. A leader recovers honor more sincerely through a deep, bowing apology than through a multiyear jail term.

(*Harvard Business Review*)[1]

The cultural wellsprings of modern Korean are Shamanism, Buddhism, and Confucianism. Shamanism is indigenous to Korea, although there is some evidence that it may have originated in Siberia.

Korean cultural history

The Koreans are a separate ethnic group from the Chinese and have a distinct language, although the literati of Korean society in ancient times learnt the language of their Chinese neighbour and assimilated many Chinese words into their own language.

The Gija Joseon state (1120–194 BC) was founded in the twelfth century BC following the arrival of the legendary sage Gija, but details of its existence are a matter of controversy among historians. The first extant written historical record of this period, known as Gojoseon, can be found from the early seventh century BC. At around the time of its founding, it is believed that there was an infusion of Chinese culture following the founding of a colony in Pyongyang by Chinese scholar Ki-tze (Kija). By around 100 BC, Chinese cultural influence had extended to neighbouring Lolang and exerted some influence over Korean tribes in the region.

Various kingdoms in the Korean peninsula waxed and waned. Consolidation began when King Dongmyeong (58–19 BC), also known by his birth name, Jumong, united Goguryeo in the north. A hero of Korean legend with magical archery skills, his fight to prevent Korea from becoming a Chinese vassal state has been dramatized in the popular Korean television series *Jumong*. In 19 BC, Jumong's second wife, Soseono, left Goguryeo and headed southwest to a region that includes modern-day Seoul, and established the kingdom of Paekche (Baekje). A third kingdom, Shilla (Silla), was founded later in 59 BC by Bak Hyeokgeose at the ancient city of Gyeongju (Kyongju) in the southeast. This completed the establishment of the Three Kingdoms (76 BC–AD 668) comprising Shilla, Paekche, and Goguryeo.

They were constantly at war for centuries, and peace did not arrive until Shilla triumphed in 668 with support from the Chinese. The country was united under one ruler in the glorious Shilla dynasty (668–935).

From Shilla to Choson

A single culture and language developed with Kyongju as its ancient capital. Korea remained united as a sovereign state for over twelve centuries, enjoying steady social and economic advancement. The Shilla dynasty overlapped with the culturally vibrant Tang dynasty in China from which it absorbed Confucianism and adopted characters for writing. The dynasty adopted Buddhism as its religion, while Confucianism became the dominant political ideology for state administration and the moral code of the people.

Rebellions in outer territories weakened the Shilla state, leading to the establishment of the Koryo (Goryeo) dynasty (935–1392). Printing using movable type was invented, and the period saw the flowering of fine ceramic pottery. Invasion by the Mongols led to their occupation from 1231–1356. Following the fall of the Mongols and the end of the Yuan dynasty in China in 1368, the impetus for a fresh beginning in Korea led to the rise and establishment of the Choson (Joseon) dynasty (1392–1910) with its capital in Seoul.

Confucianism was established as the official religion and would exert a lasting influence in Korea. The country invented its own alphabet to replace Chinese characters. In 1592, the Japanese invaded and an eight-year war followed, at the end of which they were repelled with Chinese aid. Korea went into isolation and became known as the "Hermit Kingdom," maintaining relations principally only with China. In 1637, following their conquest of China, the Manchus invaded Korea and turned it into a vassal state of China under Qing rule.

During the Choson era, Korean society was stratified into four castes: scholars (*yangban*), merchants, labourers, and "grave diggers." Most *yangban* (Figure 6.1) could read and write Chinese, collected rent and taxes, and strove to be Confucian scholars. Placing the *yangban* at the apex of the social pyramid closely followed Chinese political ideology, which treasured scholars entrusted by the emperor in the administration of the country.

Modern times

At the end of the Choson dynasty, following the resurgence of Japanese militarism and rise as an imperialistic power, the Russo-Japanese War (1905–1906) broke out.

FIGURE 6.1 A *yangban* in scholarly robes[2]

Japanese forces marched through Korea to attack Manchuria, and by 1910, they annexed Korea. During the Japanese occupation (1910–1945), the Confucian lite-rati in Korea struggled against Japanese cultural repression. The Japanese language was taught in Korean schools in an attempt to displace native Korean culture. The Confucian ideal of *ch'ung-hyo* (encompassing loyalty to state and filial piety) was propagated in the context of loyalty to the Japanese state. The Confucians resisted this by emphasizing Korean nationalism over loyalty to the state.[3]

In 1945, after World War II, Koreans were divided into two countries as the result of a deal between war partners Russia and the United States. In 1950, a powerful and well-armed North Korean army swept through the south, marking the first phase of the bloody Korean War. World War II hero General Douglas MacArthur defied both President Truman's orders and stern warnings from China, and made the fatal move of crossing the Yalu River into Chinese territory. This immediately drew China into the conflict, inflicting a devastating defeat on the US and South Korean forces, driving North Korean forces almost to the southern end of the Korean peninsula. MacArthur was unceremoniously sacked. Fierce fighting contin-ued with a heavy toll on lives, until it came to a standstill in 1953. An armistice was signed, to the chagrin of the hitherto invincible US army.

After the war, North Korea adopted Marxist ideology and Confucian ethics declined, except for the authoritarian power structure of ancient Confucian societies.

In South Korea, Western cultural influences grew. A large section of the popula-tion converted to Christianity, rising rapidly to 30 percent by the early twenty-first century. But even among Christians, Confucian values continue to set the standard of proper conduct within the social structure of South Koreans. Debates on how best to incorporate the deeply rooted Confucian tradition into Christianity have continued since the late twentieth century.[4]

Korean culture and management

Korean culture's similarity to Chinese culture lies mainly in the common elements of Buddhism and Confucianism. Shamanism is indigenous to Korea, as much as Daoism is to China.

Shamanism

Shamanism is the spiritual and intellectual basis upon which all later religions traditions would be built, and is deeply embedded in Korean culture with all its paradoxes.[5] Even young Koreans who claim they know nothing about shamanism may not be aware that its beliefs are already be deeply planted into their subconscious through daily life practices and family upbringing. For example, it would not be unusual for a Christian woman to visit a shaman to seek success for her husband's new enterprise or her daughter's entry into a good college.[6]

Shamanism forms part of a cosmology in the Korean collective consciousness, and can be positively viewed as contributing to social movement in modern Korea by helping to form a national identity.[7] It has facilitated the indigenization of foreign religions and ideologies such as Buddhism, Christianity, and Confucianism, in effect bridging the gap between different religious traditions in Korea.

The main tenets of Shamanism are: (1) man and spirits coexist and can be mediated through priests (or shamans); and (2) diseases are caused and regulated by spirits.

There is striking similarity in the understanding of the nature of illness in shamanism with that of Greco-Roman and Chinese medicine in antiquity. In ancient Greece and Rome, one school of thought viewed illnesses as caused by spirits, hence the existence of the "temple medicine." Sick patients would sleep in temples where the gods were believed to enter their dreams to intervene and resolve their conditions. Until the Han dynasty in China, it was also generally believed that spirits caused illnesses and mediums and chants would be used to dispel evil spirits. Such beliefs were largely dispelled when the medical classic, *Huang Di Nei Jing (The Yellow Emperor's Canon of Medicine)* appeared as a scientific document, and stated categorically that diseases were attributable to natural factors such as adverse climatic conditions and emotional imbalances.

In contemporary Korea, shamanism is also known as "shaman mudang." The mudang (Figure 6.2), often a woman, intercedes between human beings and gods, helping humans to reach such goals as great fortune, finding a life partner, the birth of a son, or good luck when moving to a new house. Chronic refractory health conditions may be healed by exorcising evil spirits. Modern Koreans who are committed to Buddhism, Christianity, or Confucianism are not averse to resorting to Shamanistic beliefs and practices to improve their chances of attaining their hearts' desires.[8]

FIGURE 6.2 Mudang officiating a shaman ceremony[9]

Confucianism in modern Korea

By most accounts, Confucianism reached the peak of its influence in state admin-istration during the Choson era, which was abruptly ended by the Japanese annexation of Korea in 1910. After World War II, Confucian ethics continued to be deeply embedded in Korean culture, but its political role in state governance underwent changes with each ruling regime. In earlier decades following the war, it was treated at times as a threat to the ruling regime, but, more often, as providing an ideological buttress to the exercise of autocratic rule. From the 1980s, young intel-lectuals rebelled against the elitism inherent in Confucian traditions by rejecting the *yangban* culture and wearing down the exalted status of the descendants of the upper Confucian class.

The increasing encroachment of Western culture led to socio-cultural change and the erosion of traditional values. This encouraged the revival of Confucianism as a value system for a moral society based on benevolence and proper conduct.[10]

During the 1997 Asian financial crisis, people lined up in the streets to contribute gold to sustain the economy and avert a crash, a phenomenon that writer Hahm Chai-bong attributed to community values derived from Confucianism.[11] Tu Wei-ming likewise argued that Confucian values of the common good and hard work without immediate reward explained Korea's rapid recovery from the 2009 financial crisis, achieving 6 percent growth in 2010 while most of the developed world stagnated.[12]

At the personal level, while individual freedom has gained currency as a result of Western cultural influence, it has not necessarily been at the expense of group values. As Chan observes, the existence of any functional social system results from

FIGURE 6.3 *Chugyedaeje*, a Confucian ritual ceremony in autumn in Jeju[13]

the individual's "inner deliberation."[14] Korean society is not anti-individualistic just on account of emphasizing communitarian welfare. Instead, Koreans know that they have personal freedoms to choose their individual courses in life, but this must always be within the authority of society's traditions if social harmony is to be maintained.[15]

At the social level, Confucian influence is particularly evident in contemporary South Korean family life, as group-oriented living, Confucian rituals (for example, *Chugyedaeje*, as shown in Figure 6.3) and ancestor memorial services are commonly seen today. But it appears most entrenched in patriarchal authority and privilege in business organizations, of which the most prominent are the powerful *chaebols*.

Confucianism and *chaebols* in Korean business

Confucianism hierarchical authority and group values were very much at the heart of state ideology when *chaebols*, South Korea's unique kind of conglomerates, were conceived and developed to spearhead the country's recovery from World War II and the Korean War.

The *chaebols* are a form of family-led South Korean conglomerates. The word *chaebol* come from the combination of *chae* (財) for wealth and *bol* (閥) for group, suggesting a group with substantial wealth resources.[16]

They fill up the list of the largest and most powerful companies in the country, and include household names like Samsung, Hyundai, SK, LG, Lotte, and Hanjin.

Today, the top ten *chaebols* contribute to about half of the Korean economy, with Samsung alone accounting for about 17 percent of GDP.[17]

Most *chaebols* gained prominence after the country was ravaged by the Korean War. The development of the *chaebol* system accelerated under Park Chung-hee's presidency (1961–1979). Preferential treatment was given to certain companies to promote economic growth. They were carefully selected, based on performance and potential, and awarded military contracts and government projects in the construction industry. They were also granted tax concessions, export subsidies, and, most important of all, financing with the government acting as guarantor.

Chaebols are unlike conglomerates in the West, which are subject to corporate governance rules and watched over by independent directors. They are also distinct from the *keiretsu* in Japan, which revolve around a bank that provides capital and financing, although *chaebols* may have – in the past – drawn inspiration from Japan's *zaibatsu* in Japan (the precursors of the *keiretsu*). A *chaebol* is controlled by one family led by a Confucian patriarchal figure. The immediate and extended family of this patriarch are trusted to hold strategic positions in key units of the conglomerate. Succession to the patriarch is usually reserved for one of his sons.

Korean business culture is characterized by what Fukuyama terms a low level of trust by family corporate leaders for their employees.[18] High trust countries are the United States, the United Kingdom, Germany, and, interestingly, Japan, whose *zaibatsus* were models for *chaebols* when they were first formed. The family patriarch from the Tokugawa era in Japan gave way to elite professional managers, but has persisted to the present day in South Korea, and is a source of concern to corporate governance watchdogs, and an object of resentment to younger Koreans exposed to more liberal Western cultural norms.[19]

The *chaebols* played a major role in nation-building in the early decades after the Korean War. By having to deal with only the heads of some two dozen large *chaebols*, the government had its fingers on the pulse of Korean business, and was placed in a position to formulate and promote industrial policies through them. Further control was exercised through the banks that financed the *chaebols*, at least until the 1980s when their multinational reach rendered them more independent of the state. Corporate governance declined as a result. Under Kim Young-sam's rule (1993–1997), regulatory controls were tightened and several *chaebol* heads were prosecuted for corruption. During the 1997 Asian financial crisis, sixteen out of the top thirty *chaebols* collapsed and many of the rest were bailed out with government assistance, further tightening the state's rein over them.[20]

Leaders of *chaebols* continue to exercise strong influence over government policies. Because of their wealth and ubiquitous networks, they are cultivated by politicians seeking to leverage their influence, sometimes benefitting from their financial largesse. This has led to many corporate and political scandals.

In 2008, Samsung chairman Lee Kun-hee was convicted of tax evasion, breach of trust, and running a slush fund for political ends. He went to jail briefly, but was released promptly with a pardon from President Lee Myung-bak. This was his second pardon, having been convicted of bribing a South Korean president in 1997 and then pardoned. In 2007, Hyundai Chairman Chung Mong-koo was found guilty of bribing officials and embezzlement. The victory for transparency and rule of law was short-lived. Chung had his three-year jail term suspended in 2008, and received a full pardon from President Lee Myung-bak.[21]

In March 2017, South Korean President Park Geun-hye was removed from office, in part because of accusations that she helped a friend, Choi Soon-sil, pressure companies into making donations to non-profit organizations controlled by Choi. She also allegedly gave Choi access to secret government documents.[22] The high-profile trial palliated public anger over corruption engendered by the pernicious influence of big business. But it scarcely eradicated the source that compromised President Park, which lay in the hands of those who wielded wealth.

Public tolerance for vulgar displays of wealth and influence by family members of *chaebol* leaders has been worn thin, erupting in the infamous "nut rage" caper that broke in 2015. It was a kind of catharsis for younger Koreans bitterly resentful of this unsavoury side of Confucian hierarchical culture. Ms Cho, daughter of the chairman of Hanjin Group's Korean Air, was found guilty of violating aviation law after a high-profile trial. Displeased with a flight attendant who served her nuts in an improper manner, she forced him to kneel in contrition, and drove another out of the airplane just before it took off.[23]

As *chaebols* grew into sprawling empires with many and diverse business units within each conglomerate, it became impossible for one family to have enough shareholdings in all the key units within the *chaebol* to exercise effective control. Over time, complicated crossholding structures emerged such that, with only a small fraction of shares in these units, the family could still control the entire conglomerate like the head of an octopus with multiple tentacles.

After the 1990s, the foreign investment community exerted pressure on *chaebols* to show more transparent holding structures, leading, in one case, to the restructuring of the LG Group to a Western-style holding, making it harder for the governance lapses plaguing this group in the past to take root.

But Samsung was so financially powerful and politically well-connected that it proved resilient to these pressures. Its strategic businesses units, ranging from mobile phones to life insurance, presented a challenge for the financial analyst to figure out. Therein lay the seeds of a debacle that was to unravel in the ineptly handled attempt to install the scion of Samsung's ruling Lee family to succeed his father in 2015.

Trouble in paradise: succession planning in Samsung[24]

As the largest *chaebol* in Korea, accounting for 15–20 percent of the country's GDP, Samsung's dominance in the national economy has sometimes earned South Korea the dubious moniker of The Republic of Samsung.[25] In many ways, it is representative of not only the success and global power of Korean *chaebols*, but also of the corruption and slack corporate governance that surrounds them.

Following the ageing patriarch Lee Kun-hee's heart attack in 2014, moves were afoot to replace him with his son Jay Y. Lee, scion of the Lee family (Figure 6.4).

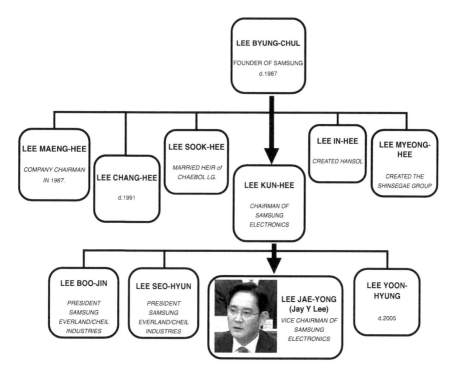

FIGURE 6.4 Samsung family relationships[26]

But given the intricate web of some seventy companies in the group with no formal holding company and board of directors, it would require some deft corporate engineering to install him as the new chief with effective control over the principal operating units of the group.

His substantial holdings and effective control over one of the major components, Cheil Industries, seemed to hold the key. Cheil held stakes in strategic units Samsung Life and Samsung C&T, the latter having a controlling stake in the star of the group, Samsung Electronics. A merger of Cheil and Samsung C&T would place most of the key strategic assets of the group within his reach and cement his position as the new leader of the *chaebol*.

On 26 May 2015, the sensational announcement of the proposed merger broke out through the wires of global investors in the Samsung companies. New York–based hedge fund Elliott Management, which had earlier acquired a 7.1 percent strategic stake in Samsung C&T (henceforth SCT), was not pleased. Elliott insisted that the proposed deal grossly undervalued their stake in SCT. The board of SCT hurriedly convened a meeting to persuade investors of the merits of the deal. But it was apparent to most that this was a devilish scheme to benefit the Lee family at the expense of shareholders of SCT and its affiliate Samsung Electronics.

The National Pension Service (NPS), which runs Korea's National Pension fund and held a 10.15 percent stake in SCT as well as a significant stake in Cheil, declared that it was not conflicted as it held shares in both entities. As such, the NPS supported the deal, setting the stage for the national furore over corporate governance at the country's most important private and public institutions.

But foreign pleas for corporate governance failed to swing minority shareholders, who were offered walnuts and watermelons at the decisive shareholder meeting on 17 July 2015, which approved the merger.[27] It was a pyrrhic victory for Jay Lee as public disquiet over the decline of corporate governance in the Cheil-SCT merger may have been a factor in Lee being charged and found guilty of national influence peddling. He was sentenced to five years' jail in 2017. But in a stunning reversal, the courts reduced his jail term by half and suspended his sentence for bribery and embezzlement for four years, releasing him in February 2018 after only one year's detention.[28]

Notwithstanding the stubborn hold that powerful *chaebols* have over Korean business and politics, there are hopeful signs of changes in Samsung. The Future Strategic Office, Samsung's top policymaking body for dealing with government affairs, was disbanded and centralized decision-making devolved to affiliate companies.

The Cheil-Samsung C&T merger saga was revived after Jay Lee's release in 2018. In June 2019, tenacious prosecutors stepped up investigations of the possible involvement of senior Samsung executives in alleged accounting fraud that may have manipulated the terms of the merger between Cheil and Samsung C&T. What caught public attention was that South Korean President Moon Jai-in visited a Samsung factory in April 2019 and appeared "smiling warmly while shaking hands" with Jay Lee, applauding Samsung's ambitious spending plans which his administration would "actively aid." With a slowing national economy, speculation is rife that President Moon may be under pressure to seek help from the giant *chaebols* to make investments to stimulate the economy, hence necessitating politically expedient compromises with companies like Samsung.[29]

Given the deep Confucian roots of the powerful *chaebols*, it is unlikely that radical changes will take place quickly in a country so steeped in a traditional culture of respect for patriarchal authority and the political influence of these enormously wealthy families.

Notes

1 Chun (2017).
2 Émile Bourdaret. (1904). "Photograph of Yang-bane en voyage" [A travelling yangban]. Scanned from *En Corée*. Paris: la Librairie Plon, p. 296. Uploaded to Wikimedia *Commons by Bzhqc on 18 April 2019. Available online at https://commons.wikimedia.org/w/index. php?curid=78134916.*
3 Kim (1996), p. 216.
4 Ibid., p. 204.

5 Kim (2003).
6 Kim (1996), p. 204.
7 Kim (2006), pp. 46–7. For more information on Shamanism in Korea, see Kim (2006), Chapter 2, "The search for meaning in Korean culture," specifically the subsection titled "The core cultural traditions: Shamanism and Confucianism," pp. 44–54.
8 *New World Encyclopedia* (2018).
9 Photograph of Dangun Shaman Ceremony by Dan Davies, distributed under GNU Free Documentation Licence, Version 1.2 or any later version published by the Free Software Foundation. Uploaded to *New World Encyclopedia* at www.newworldencyclopedia.org/entry/File:Dangun_Celebration_Mudang_2.jpg.
10 Kim (1996), pp. 222–7.
11 Hahm Chaibong's remarks are cited in Power (2012). He is president of the Asan Institute for Policy Studies and co-author of *Confucianism for the Modern World*.
12 Tu's remarks are cited in Power (2012).
13 Photograph by Joonghijung. https://commons.wikimedia.org/wiki/File:Korean_Confucianism-Chugyedaeje-01.jpg.
14 See Chan (2002), pp. 281–310.
15 Śleziak (2013).
16 Murillo and Sung (2013), p. 3.
17 *Pulse* (2018).
18 Fukuyama (1995). Fukuyama's list of low trust countries includes China, Taiwan, France, and Italy.
19 See, for example, Pesek (2013) and Hazlehurst (2013).
20 Cho (2015).
21 Tharoor (2010).
22 Chun (2017).
23 BBC News (2014).
24 This section uses information from the Harvard Business School Case 9–117–036 by Yu and Gray (2017).
25 Yu and Gray (2017), p. 2.
26 This line chart of family relationships in Samsung has been constructed by the author from information derived from Shen (2015). I have also included a picture of Jay Lee in my chart. Photograph of Jay Lee (Lee Jae-yong) in 2016, uploaded to Wikimedia Commons on 8 December 2016 by KBS, distributed under the Creative Commons Attribution 3.0 Unported Licence at https://commons.wikimedia.org/wiki/File:Lee_Jae-yong_in_2016.jpg.
27 *BBC News* (2015).
28 Kim (2018); *The Straits Times* (2018).
29 *The Economist* (2019).

References

BBC News. (2014). "'Nut Rage': Korean Air Ex-executive Cho Hyun-ah Detained," 30 December. Available online at www.bbc.com/news/world-asia-30636204. Accessed 9 April 2019.
BBC News. (2015). "Shareholders Approve Controversial Samsung C&T Merger," 17 July. Available online at www.bbc.com/news/business-33546434. Accessed 9 April 2019.
Daniel A. Bell and Hahm Chaibong (eds.). (2003). *Confucianism for the Modern World*. Cambridge: Cambridge University Press.
Joseph Chan. (2002). "Moral Autonomy, Civil Liberties, and Confucianism." *Philosophy East and West* 52 (3): 281–310. Available online at www.jstor.org/stable/1400320. Accessed 23 July 2019.

Cho Mu-hyun. (2015). "The Chaebols: The Rise of South Korea's Conglomerates." *CNET*, 6 April. Available online at www.cnet.com/news/the-chaebols-the-rise-of-south-koreas-mighty-conglomerates/. Accessed 23 July 2019.

Rosa Chun. (2017). "Samsung, Shame, and Corporate Atonement." *Harvard Business Review*, 17 May. Available online at https://hbr.org/2017/05/samsung-shame-and-corporate-atonement. Accessed 23 July 2019.

The Economist. (2019). "Some Guns Blazing: South Korea's Left-Wing President Loses His Zeal to Humble Big Business," 22 June. Available online at www.economist.com/asia/2019/06/22/south-koreas-left-wing-president-loses-his-zeal-to-humble-big-business. Accessed 23 July 2019.

Francis Fukuyama. (1995). *Trust: The Social Virtues and the Creation of Prosperity*. New York: The Free Press.

Jeremy Hazlehurst. (2013). "Chaebols: King of the Conglomerates." *Campden FB*, 25 February. Available online at www.campdenfb.com/article/chaebols-kings-conglomerates. Accessed 9 April 2019.

Kim Chongho. (2003). *Korean Shamanism: The Cultural Paradox*. Aldershot, Hampshire: Ashgate.

Kim Kwong-ok. (1996). "The Reproduction of Confucian Culture in Contemporary Korea: An Anthropological Study." In Tu Wei-ming (ed.), *Confucian Traditions in East Asian Modernity: Moral Education and Economic Culture in Japan and the Four Mini-Dragons*, 202–27. Cambridge, MA: Harvard University Press.

Kyong Ju Kim. (2006). *The Development of Modern South Korea: State Formation, Capitalist Development and National Identity*. Oxon and New York: Routledge.

Sam Kim. (2018). "Samsung's Jay Y. Lee Set Free in Unexpected Court Reversal." *Bloomberg*, 5 February. Available online at www.bloomberg.com/news/articles/2018-02-05/samsung-heir-jay-y-lee-goes-free-after-court-suspends-jail-term. Accessed 9 April 2019.

David Murillo and Yun-dal Sung. (2013). "Understanding Korean Capitalism: Chaebols and their Corporate Governance." *ESADEgeo Position Paper 33*, ESADEgeo Center for *Global Economics and Geopolitics, September. Available online at http://itemsweb.esade.edu/research/esadegeo/201309Chaebols_Murillo_Sung_EN.pdf. Accessed 23 July 2019.*

New World Encyclopedia. (2018). "Korean Shamanism." Entry last modified on 24 April 2018. *Available online at www.newworldencyclopedia.org/entry/Korean_shamanism. Accessed 6 April 2019.*

William Pesek. (2013). "Breaking the Chaebols' Stranglehold on Koreans." *Straits Times*, 10 July.

John Power. (2012). "Does Confucianism Have a Role in Korea Today?" *Korea Herald*, 13 February. Available online at www.koreaherald.com/view.php?ud=20120213001231. Accessed 23 July 2019.

Pulse, by Maell Business News Korea. (2018). "Top 10 Korean Inc. Revenue Equivalent to Nearly Half of GDP," 6 September. Available online at https://pulsenews.co.kr/view.php?year=2018&no=562268. Accessed 8 April 2019.

Tomasz Śleziak. (2013). "The Role of Confucianism in Contemporary South Korean Society." *Rocznik Orietalistyczny* [Yearbook of Oriental Studies] 66 (1): 27–46.

Lucinda Shen. (2015). "Meet Samsung's Billionaire Lee Family, South Korea's Most Powerful Dynasty." *Business Insider*, 19 June. Available online at www.businessinsider.com/lee-family-power-war-for-samsung-scandals-and-bribes-2015-6. Accessed 9 April 2019.

The Straits Times. (2018). "Samsung Scion Lee Jae Yong Walks Free as South Korea Court Suspends Jail Term," 5 February. Available online at www.straitstimes.com/asia/east-asia/south-korean-appeals-court-sets-samsung-scion-jay-y-lee-free. Accessed 9 April 2019.

Ishaan Tharoor. (2010). "Chung Mong Koo, Hyundai Motor." *Time*, 10 August. Available online at http://content.time.com/time/specials/packages/article/0,28804,2009445_2009447_2009523,00.html. Accessed 9 April 2019.

Tu Wei-ming (ed.). (1996). *Confucian Traditions in East Asian Modernity: Moral Education and Economic Culture in Japan and the Four Mini-Dragons.* Cambridge, MA: Harvard University Press.

Gwen Yu and Tim Gray. (2017). "Succession Planning at Samsung: The Merger Formula of Cheil Industries and Samsung C&T." Harvard Business School Case 9–117–036, April. (Revised 19 June 2017).

7

DEMOCRATIC GOVERNANCE WITH SINGAPOREAN CHARACTERISTICS

We would not have made economic progress if we had not intervened on very personal matters – who your neighbour is, how you live, the noise you make, how you spit, or what language you use. We decide what is right. Never mind what the people think.
(Lee Kuan Yew, National Day Rally Speech, 1986)

Singapore's success story is a fascinating case study of how farsighted leadership, working within the rule of law and guided by Confucian principles, managed the institutions of a liberal democracy as instruments of control for a benign authoritarian state. The term "authoritarian" is used here in a neutral sense to denote a style of governance that deemphasizes personal freedoms in favour of the authority of a ruling elite. Authoritarianism can and does exist to different degrees within electoral democracies, and some are economic successes.

Singapore's social stability and efficient public services are the envy of Western leaders who lament the dysfunctional processes threatening to rip their democracies apart. The ruling People's Action Party (PAP) of Singapore has won every general election with an almost clean sweep of all parliamentary seats since Singapore became a sovereign state in 1965. Does this reflect the Machiavellian genius of founding Premier Lee Kuan Yew, whose dominating personality and political energy rallied the city-state after she was rudely ejected from Malaysia? Is Singapore a flash in the pan, as Samuel Huntington intimated when he predicted that the system that Lee put in place would not survive him?[1] Or has Singapore found a way to make a virtue of authoritarian governance and in so doing provided a model for the world to emulate?

As always, it pays first to study how culture has evolved in the country. In the case of Singapore, it is particularly relevant because of her exotic mix of ethnicities as well as her uneasy mix of British liberalism with Confucian values.

Stamford Raffles of the East India Company colonized Singapore for the British in 1819. He saw the value in the island's strategic position at the tip of the Malayan archipelago along one of the key shipping trade routes of the world. For centuries, this had already been a node for trade and the transmission of cultures. The British exploited it further for their own gains, but helped create one of the greatest ports of the world in the process.[2]

Credit for the economic success of contemporary Singapore goes to the island state's own founding fathers. They shook off colonial rule by merging the island into the new state of Malaysia, only to be thrown out two years later and left behind with a struggling economy. Her plight was exacerbated soon after by the abrupt withdrawal of the British naval base that had been an important source of employment for the locals.

With her back to the wall and her survival in peril, the little new state with no natural resources drew on the surging patriotism and political will of an unusually talented and dedicated group. Besides Lee, the founding fathers included economic visionary Goh Keng Swee, eloquent foreign affairs minister S. Rajaratnam, manager *par excellence* Lim Kim San, and the ideological purist Toh Chin Chye, chairman of the PAP.

Before he could bring about social change and shape Singapore's future, Lee had first to gain strong control. While Singapore was under the last phase of colonial rule, Lee's faction of the PAP had formed an alliance with the radical left to gain power in 1959. Thereafter, leftists became increasingly alienated from Lee's capitalistic-leaning policies. In 1961, they split off to form the opposition Barisan Socialis, threatening Lee's control of the PAP. On 2 February 1963, a covert security operation codenamed "Operation Coldstore" arrested 113 people in one sweep and detained them without trial under the Preservation of Public Service Security Ordinance. The exercise was officially "aimed at crippling the Communist open front organisation," but it also decimated the Barisan Socialis as a political organization.[3]

This left the PAP unchallenged, and set the stage for its social engineering and bold public policies that would ultimately result in the creation of an economic miracle. By 2015, when she celebrated her fiftieth anniversary as a nation, Singapore enjoyed a per capita income that placed her among the top five in the world, exceeding that of Britain.

Social and political Confucianism

Singapore's success has justly been attributed to strict governance and the pragmatism of its founding fathers. These qualities take the form of strong leadership, an elite civil service, an open economy, and low levels of corruption. Premier Lee Kuan Yew practised a brand of Confucianism which comprised paternalism and a mix of persuasion and Machiavellianism to deal with rivals. It won him international admiration and recognition as a statesman.

Confucianism was not evident in the young man, who had recently finished his studies in Law in England and spoke with a newly minted English accent that caught the attention of Chinese premier Zhou En Lai at the Bandung Conference of 1954. Zhou remarked that he was "like a banana – yellow of skin, white underneath."[4] Neither did it help Lee's image that he earned the dubious accolade of being "the best bloody Englishman east of the Suez" from British foreign secretary George Brown in the 1960s.[5]

It was only in his later years that Lee more openly acknowledged Confucian influences in his life. In a conversation with former German chancellor Helmut Schmidt about his upbringing, he extolled Confucian family values and, perhaps in a Freudian slip, prized loyalty to the Emperor as well:

Schmidt: When did you actually become Confucian?

Lee: I have already asked myself this question too. I think I was educated as a Confucian. Concerning family and values [*sic*]. There is a Chinese proverb which goes like this: If you care for yourself, you care for your family; if you are loyal to the Emperor, the country will be successful. This means, first of all, that you need to care for yourself and be a gentleman. This is a basic need. Every individual should try to be a gentleman.[6]

At the height of his powers, Lee was sometimes called "Emperor Lee" in jest, a reference to his imperious style and ruthless tactics. But most Singaporeans of the older generation accepted his heavy hand as the price to pay for higher living standards.

Lee's influence carried over to the two prime ministers who succeeded him, and whom he watched over from a mentorship perch in the cabinet. The PAP's total dominance has enabled it to make constitutional changes that helped embed the Confucian ideology of the party within the country's governance, thereby consolidating its grip on power.

Characterizing Lee's authoritarian style as a way to effective government, Michael Barr sees his emphasis on grooming a well-educated governing elite as the perfect marriage of Confucian humanism with Legalism. "Legalist principles provided Lee with the art of statecraft, while Confucianism justifies the rule of the elite."[7] While this interpretation of Lee's methods fits nicely with traditional Chinese political theories, a more realistic view is that the man was simply a pragmatist interested in results, with little regard for ideology.

Authoritarian Confucianism

In the early years of nation-building, Lee's attempts at fostering Confucian values were not successful. In the 1980s, after phasing out Chinese-medium schools and Chinese-language-based Nanyang University, he expressed concern over the rapid decline in Confucian virtue stemming from the diminished use of the Chinese language and its store of moral precepts conveyed through idioms, aphorisms and narratives. In a hasty attempt to bring back these virtues, he set up the Institute of East Asian Philosophies in 1983 and appointed the noted Confucian scholar Wu Teh Yao as its head. But the scholastic approach bore little fruit as Confucian

FIGURE 7.1 President Ong Teng Cheong (left) and PM Lee Kuan Yew (extreme right) in Suzhou, China, for discussions on the Singapore-Suzhou Industrial Park (1993)

Source: Photograph from the author's personal collection

values are not transmitted by instruction, but mainly by example through the conduct of teachers and parents. The Institute ceased to be a centre for propagating Confucian values.[8] Lee noted Confucian practices in visits to China (Figure 7.1).

Subsequent efforts to promote Confucianism through legislation were greeted with scepticism. Singapore introduced a law in 1994 entitling all people aged sixty years and above who are unable to fend for themselves to claim maintenance from their children.[9] Simon Leys points out the irony that rites (*li*) become laws only when morality has completely broken down. Hence, instituting duty through ordinances is an admission of a society's moral failure.[10]

> This paradox seems to have escaped a more activist school of modern Confucianism; the government of Singapore, in its naive but somewhat misguided enthusiasm, recently enacted *laws* to enforce Confucian morality: if they feel neglected by unfilial children, parents can now take their unfilial offspring to court![11]

Confucianism took root in Singapore in ways that even the visionary Lee had not adequately understood in earlier years – by transmission from parent to child at home. Today, Confucian virtues are behind generous education budgets; the relentless pursuit of excellence, meritocracy, subsidised housing, and healthcare; and harsh punishment, including public shaming for uncivil behaviour. The extent of Confucian paternalism earned Singapore the reputation of being a nanny state.

Disdain for liberal democracy

Besides being promoted as a system of personal ethics for common folk in Singapore, Confucianism has also served as a political ideology. At the centre of Confucian humanism is the wise ruler who governs by using good people rather than by laws. Lee recognized this point even as a young legislator at the opposition benches in 1957, as he quipped: "If people have lost faith completely in their democratic institutions because they cannot find men of calibre to run them, then, however good the system, it perishes. Ultimately it is the men who run the system that come to life."[12]

Nonetheless, scholars of Singaporean politics have noted the authoritarian nature of Confucian political ideology. Chan Heng Chee's 1976 study concluded that British colonial rule based on centralized authoritarian decision-making and the Confucian political culture of the ethnic Chinese were key determining factors for one-party dominance.[13] Chua Beng Huat theorized that the retreat of liberal democracy during the latter part of Lee's rule resulted from communitarian values that evolved from "concepts of Confucianism and the so-called 'collectivism' of Asian traditions."[14]

By the 1990s, Lee's disdain for democracy was articulated with even greater conviction, for he declared:

> With few exceptions, democracy has not brought good government to new developing countries. . . . What Asians value may not necessarily be what Americans or Europeans value. Westerners value the freedoms and liberties of the individual. As an Asian of Chinese cultural background, my values are for a government which is honest, effective and efficient.[15]

Earlier, Lee had given an interview to Fareed Zakaria in *Foreign Affairs*, during the course of which he placed emphasis on culture as a determinant of economic success, and denigrated the American culture of violence in schools and over-dependence on government to solve economic problems to sustain social stability.[16] He was unfazed by criticisms of authoritarianism. For example, former South Korean President Kim Dae Jung charged that Lee's views were not only unsupportable, but also self-serving. The Nobel peace laureate argued passionately that democracy had a long tradition in Asia and would eventually re-emerge as the most common form of government in the region:

> In Lee's Singapore, the government stringently regulates individuals; actions . . . to an Orwellian extreme of social engineering. . . . The proper way to cure the ills of industrial societies is not to impose the terror of a police state but to emphasize ethical education, give high regard to spiritual values. . . .

The best proof that democracy can work in Asia is the fact that, despite the stubborn resistance of authoritarian rulers like Lee, Asia has made great strides toward democracy.[17]

Lee's distrust of liberal democracy showed in tough politics vis-a-vis adversaries and dissidents. In "Operation Spectrum" in 1987, sixteen activists, mainly young Catholic activists who had lobbied for the rights of poorer workers, were apprehended in a late night sweep; another six were arrested a month later. Allegedly under duress and torture, they confessed to being part of a "Marxist conspiracy" to de-stabilize Singapore.[18]

The Marxist thesis was hardly credible at a time when communism was no longer in vogue, prompting historian Mary Turnbull to call the government narrative a "myth."[19] A senior member of the cabinet S. Dhanabalan reportedly resigned over the saga. The government account was repudiated thirty years later in personal testimonies of the protagonists in the book *1987*.[20] The book was discreetly ignored by the authorities and the Singapore mainstream media.

After Operation Spectrum, the Maintenance of Religious Harmony Act was passed, empowering the Minister for Home Affairs to take action against religious leaders whose words were deemed to threaten religious harmony. But the Act also banned religions leaders from politics, greatly strengthening the government's control over their political activities, thereby preventing them from becoming sources of social instability.[21]

Lee's views on governance for Singapore were vividly captured in the political biography *Lee Kuan Yew: Hard Truths to Keep Singapore Going*, in which his distrust of liberal democracy and his faith in an authoritarian ruling elite were spelt out for the guidance of future generations of leaders.[22] It has remained the received wisdom of good governance among the current generation of leaders.

Economic management and social engineering in a Confucian state

Despite Western contempt for authoritarian regimes, few dispute the fact that Singapore's success could have been achieved without a combination of strong leadership, top-down governance with pragmatism, meritocracy, an elite civil service, an open economy, and low levels of corruption.

Notwithstanding its support for free markets, the government has never hesitated to intervene in key parameters such wages, interest rates, money supply, and exchange rates when necessary. Industrial policy is a staple of the island's economic management, despite its many ideological critics in the West.

But the visible guiding hand sometimes made mistakes. Singapore, in recent years, may have failed to differentiate between expansion and growth. Former Economic Development Board chairman Ngiam Tong Dow opined in 2011 that Singapore's GDP increases of the previous two decades were due largely to population expansion rather than productivity growth, supported by the import of large numbers of foreign employees.[23] The influx of foreign workers and professionals may have also led to feelings of insecurity among citizens who had lost their jobs to foreigners.

For Singapore to remain competitive and quickly adaptable to changing world economic environments, an authoritarian regime ruled by the sagacious and benevolent philosopher kings of Plato's *Republic* has been the ruling paradigm. The ability to implement long-term economic plans for the country was helped by the dominance of the ruling People's Action Party. This gave the government a free hand to carry out long-term policies, often unpopular ones, to secure economic growth and social stability.

Social engineering took many forms, including the prohibition of racial enclaves in public housing estates, costly fines for littering, and the banning of the sales of chewing gum. Lee was a believer in eugenics, a view not shared by many establishment Singaporeans. Conceding that producing high economic achievers may be the result of both nature and nurture, he asked that "some system of incentives and disincentives must be found to make sure that with each succeeding generation, standards of education and skill, levels of performance and achievement, would rise both as a result of nature and of nurture."[24] The graduate mother scheme, by which women who had university degrees were given financial incentives to procreate more, was unsuccessful and eventually dropped.

A forced high savings rate sees the average Singaporean put a big part of their income (about 30 percent for the lower to middle income) into the Central Provident Fund (CPF). The funds may be used to purchase public housing from the Housing and Development Board (HDB), where some 80 percent of Singaporeans live. The twin agencies of the CPF and the HDB lend the government enormous control over Singaporean lives. This is enhanced further by various grassroots organizations administered by the People's Association (PA). The PA closely monitors the habits and sentiments of HDB residents and conducts activities to promote a better understanding of government policies.

The introduction of Town Councils in 1988 placed the running of HDB estates directly under the Members of Parliament of various electoral constituencies. Non-PAP MPs have had a poor track record operating these town councils, as revealed by the recent travails of new MPs in the Aljunied Group Representation Constituency (GRC) that fell to the Workers' Party in 2011. These MPs had little experience in estate management and could not count on experienced managing agents, who did not seem to be readily available to provide services, preoccupied as they were with PAP-run town councils.

The independence of the judiciary is sacrosanct. Allegations that it is not independent or that it rules in favour of the ruling party in political disputes are dealt with vigorously by the law.

The Elections Department reports directly to the office of the prime minister. Alternative parties complain that this takes away its neutrality, giving it free rein to gerrymander electoral boundaries to the advantage of the PAP. Frequent changes in electoral boundaries seem to lend support to this perception. In five consecutive general elections, I voted in four different constituencies, even though I never changed my address over that period.[25]

The media was reined in to support the government in nation-building.[26] The former chief editor of the *Straits Times*, Cheong Yip Seng, provides a revealing account of Lee's rationale for limiting press freedom whereby the custodial responsibility of government for the country's welfare and security must take precedence over all else, including press freedom: "The question for the Singapore media was this: who voted for you that you should be entitled to speak for the voters, or tear down government policies?"[27]

Gathering clouds

Success breeds higher expectations from each succeeding generation. The pioneer generation, who are now in their seventies and beyond, have by and large been loyal to the PAP. But Singapore Millennials are a different lot, an exciting generation with the daring to experiment with their careers and the audacity to risk changes in the proven political formula for the maintenance of the country's prosperity.

However, the issue of rising equality is a concern that cuts across all generations.

Inequality

Distribution of income has been a nagging economic issue. Inequality has become a hot-button national issue particularly following a much-cited study by sociologist Teo You Yenn that contrasted the hardships of family life, schooling, parenting, and housing among the poor with the creature comforts enjoyed by the upper middle class and elite, and called out the shortcomings of the Singapore's welfare policies.[28]

Despite significant transfers through taxation and subsidy measures, Singapore's GINI coefficient stubbornly remains among the highest in the world. Concerned for the unskilled labour wages that went along with cheap imported labour, economist and former chairman of the National Wages council Lim Chong Yah raised eyebrows when he called for "wage shock therapy" aimed at forcibly increasing worker wages to narrow the yawning income gap between rich and poor.[29] Tommy Koh, a former director of the Institute of Policy Studies, has urged for the introduction of minimum wages.

These challenges notwithstanding, the Singapore economy has grown at an impressive rate in the last ten years. However, anticipation of sharply increased spending on healthcare and transportation infrastructure has led the government to announce a likely increase in the goods and services tax in the near future. Already living in one of the costliest cities in the world, Singaporeans worry about how the jobs and incomes of their children will cope with the high cost of living.

Freedom

There is concern, even among establishment figures, that limited press freedom can repress creativity and entrepreneurship. One of the most notable among these is

Mano Sabnani, the former chief editor of the *Business Times*, and managing editor of *The Straits Times*, who muses about "nation-building journalism." His memoirs argue that the future economy will not tie in well with a model of authoritarian control: "A vibrant landscape of innovation can only happen with a free press. . . . It is simply impossible . . . to have an innovative society that is not intellectually open."[30]

A similar view is held by Malaysian tycoon Robert Kuok, a Raffles College class-mate and personal friend of Lee Kuan Yew, who once counselled Lee that a nanny state kills enterprise and entrepreneurship:

> About five years ago, in 2010, he wrote me a letter asking for my candid views. He wanted to know why he always found Hong Kong full of business activity and people with strong enterprising spirit. . . . I told him that he had straightjacketed too many of his people in his zeal and impatience to build up Singapore quickly. There was genius in them, but they could not move. I told him to take a pair of scissors and cut them loose.[31]

But such pessimism may yet be proven wrong. A vibrant culture of entrepreneur-ship seems to be growing among the Millennials. Many seem little concerned about building stable careers, and do not hesitate to start new business ventures and social enterprises in search of their dreams. Apparently, venture and creativity in business is not necessarily repressed by benign authoritarian governance. The potential ills of authoritarian governance may have to be sought elsewhere.

The natural aristocracy and its discontents

An almost unavoidable result of Confucian society and meritocracy is elitism. A thousand years ago, the Song dynasty in China saw the rise of the scholar-gentry class. Regardless of their family backgrounds, scholars who excelled in the com-petitive imperial examinations (*keju*) were appointed officials. With the power of officialdom came high remuneration and the means to become wealthy landowners.

The term "natural aristocracy" gained currency in Singapore after it was used on several occasions by Lee's eldest son and the current Prime Minister Lee Hsien Loong. In a recent interview with CNN he asserted, "If you don't have a cer-tain natural aristocracy in the system, people who are respected because they have earned that and we level everything down to the lowest common denominator, then I think society will lose out."[32] This was seized upon by social media as glorifying the privileged class. It was not helped by the fact the little island state's cabinet min-isters are, by a wide margin, the highest paid in the world.

But if elitism is not much loved in Singapore, some in the West see its merit. David Brooks of the *New York Times* saw fit to recommend it to Americans, not-ing that "in places like Singapore and China, the best students are ruthlessly culled for government service." Western democracies, he argued, should emulate "Lee Kuan Yew's means to achieve Jeffersonian ends – to become less democratic at the national level."[33] Brooks was advocating meritocracy over popularity as the basis for choosing government leaders.

Most Singaporeans appear willing to accept a system with power concentrated in the hands of a few as long as it gives them a good living. As law academic Eleanor Wong points out, "Singaporeans want a monolithic government. . . . They do not believe that leaders necessarily govern better if they must answer, day to day, matter to matter, to critics. Singaporeans have freely chosen to be governed by an entrenched elite aristocracy."[34] However, Deputy Prime Minister Heng Swee Keat has acknowledged that younger Singaporeans want to see stronger opposition representation in Parliament.[35] In recent speeches, he has also encouraged Singaporeans to work *with* the government on national issues, rather than just depending on the government to work for them. Social media was quick to react, pointing out that what he had mentioned as examples for joint effort were "peripheral" issues like the environment and social mobility, rather than core concerns like immigration, CPF and the use of national reserves.[36]

East Asian Institute political scientist Lam Peng Er cautions that the new generation may not find domination by a natural aristocracy palatable. "If there is anything good or enduring about Confucianism and Asian values, then it must move beyond the parochial interests of bureaucratic authoritarian states like Singapore. . . . Asian values must be dynamic enough to be redefined by each succeeding generation." For the younger generation, he argues, Asian values must be consonant with global precepts of human rights and democracy.[37] Lam's observation may well be borne out by a new trajectory of local politics. Some smart professionals (who are not beholden to the government for security of tenure in their careers) and entrepreneurs (who do not depend on government largesse to succeed in business) increasingly espouse Western liberal values. They can potentially break the grip of the Confucian state governance.

But are the naysayers too hard on their own government? While the island may fare poorly in international rankings of press freedom, and while self-appointed Western guardians of the free world pour scorn on the one-party rule that is presently enjoying its sixth decade, Singapore is consistently ranked among the most competitive economies in the world.

By some measures, it even ranks well in happiness. In 2017, *National Geographic* magazine identified Singaporeans among the three happiest people in the world alongside the people of Denmark and Costa Rica. Detractors, however, may dispute the magazine's method of measuring happiness through heavy reliance on economic and social indicators rather than the feelings of the people.[38] One's sense of happiness may be determined by more intangible factors such as perceptions of inequality, crowded streets, and social pressure to excel. Hence, by other measures of happiness, Singapore ranks below many poorer countries.[39]

Stumbles

The 2011 general election saw the ruling party's share of vote shrink to 60.14 percent, representing a 6.46 percent swing against the PAP since the 2006 general election.[40] Some of the issues that contributed to the debacle surrounding this loss of votes were the sharp rise of immigration and foreign workers, and the inadequacy of housing, health, and transportation services in coping with the population increase.

Over the next four years, the government took decisive steps to remedy these problems. Many new HDB flats were completed, the subway system is undergoing major expansion, and several public hospitals came on stream. There was a notable decrease in the influx of new immigrants and foreign workers. These measures undoubtedly helped the PAP to regain nearly 9.8 percent of the popular vote. But a larger factor may have been the outpouring of national grief following the death of Lee Kuan Yew a few months earlier, and the fact that the election year had coincided with the euphoria of the country's golden jubilee celebrations.

Formidable challenges will face Singapore's future leaders. Among these, the most strenuous may be the task of maintaining Confucian governance in a highly educated populace inclined toward Western liberalism and the lure of greater personal freedoms. The Singapore government and ruling party have not been able to resist the tide of populism sweeping Western democracies. Maintaining its compact with the electorate may mean pursuing policies that require sharply increased spending on healthcare, transportation, and housing.

In answer to a question posed in a 2003 press interview regarding Huntington's prediction that the systems that he put in place would not survive him, Lee retorted that he had stepped down as prime minister thirteen years earlier and Singapore had not collapsed.[41] At the time, however, Lee was still a vigorous, eighty-year-old Senior Minister in a cabinet headed by his son. No one was under the illusion that he had ceased to exercise decisive influence.

More tellingly, when Lee finally stepped down from the cabinet in 2011 at the age of eighty-eight, there was already a growing perception of the serious decline in the quality of public services. In December 2017, a scam was uncovered in which a small group of operators managed to illegally withdraw S$40 million from the government's SkillsFuture fund. This prompted Tan Kin Lian, former presidential candidate and one-time chief executive of the powerful trades union enterprise NTUC Income, to charge Singapore meritocracy with being poorly built on mere academic credentials: "It only shows clearly the failing of our education system and the serious shortcoming of an elitist system where the people in charge refuse to engage people outside of their closed elite circle."[42]

Even the main Chinese daily, *Lianhe Zaobao*, known for its steadfast support of government policies and discreet handling of sensitive political issues, shocked readers on 1 February 2019 with a scathing editorial castigating the government of the day for the inexcusable lapses in the running of the nation's key institutions. More importantly, it pointed out that these lapses were the manifestation of a culture of "muddling along" that had taken root in key government institutions. They were symptomatic of the unwillingness of senior management to take responsibility for mistakes.

Among these lapses were the leak of the Ministry of Health's HIV Registry data affecting 16,000 individuals, and the hacking of the largest state-run healthcare group SingHealth, which resulted in the theft of 1.5 million patient records (including that of the prime minister). Five deaths of soldiers and preventable accidents had happened in eighteen months. The subway system's alarming series of breakdowns due to poor maintenance, power outages, and a postal service throwing away large amounts of mail that was too much trouble to deliver added to the litany of events that suggested a declining public service.[43]

Paradigm shift

Since the ruling PAP took charge in 1965, Singapore's population has tripled.[44] With a rapidly ageing demographic profile and a technological landscape changing at a breathtaking pace, serious questions need to be raised about the kind of leadership that can keep the country in the top league of well-managed economies. The indications are compelling that state governance needs a new paradigm.

Philosopher of science Thomas Kuhn demonstrated in his pathbreaking book *The Structure of Scientific Revolutions* that each major body of scientific theories establishes itself as a received group of beliefs, collectively known as a scientific paradigm. At some point in history, this paradigm becomes untenable because of inconsistency with observed facts. But scientists typically (and stubbornly) hang on to it, stretching explanations to account for observations that do not support the paradigm. This goes on until the weight of evidence is so overwhelming that the paradigm collapses and is replaced by a new paradigm through a *paradigm shift*.[45] A paradigm shift occurred when Ptolemy's view of the universe with the earth at the centre was replaced by theories of Copernicus and Newton. Centuries later, Newtonian theory itself was supplanted by Einstein's General Theory of Relativity.

Paradigm shifts occur also in the social sciences. Lee Kuan Yew, at the end of a remarkable career spanning more than fifty years, vigorously enunciated the governance philosophy of *Hard Truths to Keep Singapore Going* as the paradigm for continuing economic success. He was possibly unaware that Singapore may already have been at the cusp of a paradigm shift.

What would a new paradigm look like? There is yet no clear answer, and this is a fit subject for another book. But for now, one may consider some of its necessary elements. Multiracialism and secularism for political stability, freedom from corruption, and assistance for the poor and the weak are likely to remain pillars of governance. These are some of Lee's "hard truths" that are likely to remain. But the new paradigm would also have to address a number of specific issues. Some of these are of particular importance to Millennials who will make up the next generation of national leaders.

First, it would have to turn the notion of meritocracy on its head. The PAP has already acknowledged that it would look beyond academic ability, emotional intelligence, and technical competence for future leadership talent. But it also has to incorporate entrepreneurial daring and the courage to challenge conventional wisdom. Most of all, future leaders would need a deep strategic grasp of world affairs. Such wisdom does not come easily, and cannot be gained by knowledge absorption or educational training. It is more likely forged in vigorous intellectual contention, personal experience of adversity and failure, and an environment that does not constrain the mind with "hard truths." Where can these leaders be found, and will they fit in as natural aristocrats in a Confucian hierarchical society? Indeed, can Confucian values endure, given the inexorable penetration of Western culture into all aspects of Singapore life?

Second, it is inevitable that there is more talent outside the government than within. A freer press (with more than one newspaper company) and greater participation of thought leaders in debates on core national issues would help in the formulation of better policies. Such participation would be meaningful only if the government has a greater willingness to share information. Sharing information means that alternative viewpoints can be backed by study and analyses of up-to-date data, thereby weakening the government's current advantage of meeting challenges to its ideas by using information to which the other parties do not have ready and timely access. Civil servants would then have to be more resilient, and politicians would be less shielded by the cotton wool of superior access to information and a supportive press.

Third, the new paradigm will need to recognize the wish of younger voters to limit the power of the ruling party to make constitutional changes. In 2017, the constitution was changed to introduce a racial criterion and a sharply raised financial expertise requirement for presidential candidates. This caused some disquiet and was read by many in the public as a move to ensure that a candidate favoured by the ruling party would be elected without contest.[46]

Finally, the country should relinquish the notion that any party other than the ruling party (or ruling coalition) is "The Opposition." This attitude is prevalent in Britain and most of her former colonies (with the notable exception of the United States).[47] There is no reason for alternative views to be presumptively held as opposing views. In Daoist wisdom, *yin* and *yang* both restrain and support each other to maintain balance and harmony in a robust equilibrium. The ruling party and alternative parties representing different viewpoints should be seen in the same enlightened way.

Notes

1 In a 1995 speech, Samuel Huntington said, "The honesty and efficiency that Senior Minister Lee Kuan Yew has brought to Singapore will follow him into his grave." Quoted by Goh (2002) in his Marine Parade National Day Dinner speech.
2 Tan (2019).
3 Ee and Lim (1963), p. 10; Thum (2013); Hong, Poh and Tan (2013); Wade (2013).
4 Velloor (2015).
5 This remark is attributed to the British foreign secretary George Brown in the 1960s, cited in Billington (1996), p. 56; Davies (2015). Retrieved 14 April 2019.
6 Nass (2012).
7 Barr (2000), p. 215. See also Barr (2017).
8 Lee (2007).
9 Lim (2009).
10 Simon Leys is the pen name of Pierre Ryckmans, Professor of Chinese Studies at the University of Sydney from 1987 to 1993. He adopted the pen name Simon Leys to

protect his ability to continue travelling to China. See www.chinafile.com/contributors/simon-leys.

11 See Leys' (1997) translation of *The Analects of Confucius* Leys (1997).
12 Lee Kuan Yew in a speech to the Legislative Assembly 1957, cited in Bilveer Singh (2017), p. 77.
13 Chan Heng Chee (1976), pp. 229–30.
14 Chua Beng Huat (2002), Introduction p. 7. See also Chua Beng Huat (2017).
15 Lee (1992), cited in Mutalib (2004), p. 22.
16 Zakaria (1994).
17 Kim (1994), pp. 190–1. Kim's article was a response to Zakaria (1994). In trying to reconcile the two positions, Riegel (2000, pp. 75–96) observed that each leader's ideological position reflected his own historical baggage and political agenda. While that may be so, there is a more basic logical problem for either Kim or Lee to postulate single-factor reasons for high economic achievement. In reality, each country succeeds or fails owing to a complex interaction of many factors, and any attempt to simplify it to culture or democracy is likely to come to grief. We shall return to this point in Chapter 8.
18 Twenty-two young persons, many from the Catholic Church, were charged with being involved in a "Marxist conspiracy." Although they denied these charges, they signed confessions that were later recanted as they claimed to done so under duress. See Kaur (2009).

Lee commented on the saga much later in a 2011 interview quoted in Han et al. (2011), p. 245:

Q: In the 1980s, the government reacted to the involvement of the Catholic Church.
A: Yes, they were interfering in politics. If we had allowed it, then the other religious groups would also enter the political arena. . . . I put a stop to it.

19 Turnbull (2009), p. 339.
20 Chng, Low and Teo (2017).
21 According to Musa (2017): "The Act empowers the Minister for Home Affairs to issue a restraining order against any leader, official or member of any religious group or institution who causes ill feelings between different religious groups, promotes a political cause, carries out subversive activities, or excites disaffection against the President or the Government under the guise of propagating or practising a religious belief."
22 Han et al. (2011).
23 See Zhang (2011).
24 Lee (1970), p. 15.
25 I was in the Tanglin, Tanjong Pagar, Kallang-Moulmein, and Holland Bukit-Timah constituencies.
26 The Newspaper and Printing Act of 1974 required that the chief editor or the proprietor of the newspaper obtain a permit granted by the Minister of Communications and Information; it also gave the minister the power to appoint the management shareholders of all newspaper companies, effectively guaranteeing a two-thirds majority for the government in any vote on staffing decisions and the appointment of directors. A management share equals 200 ordinary shares for any resolution relating to the appointment and/or dismissal of a director or any member of the staff of a newspaper company. The number of management shares should be at least 1% of ordinary shares. This gives the government a minimum of 67% in votes on staffing and directorship decisions. A 1986 amendment to the Act allowed the government to restrict the sale or distribution of foreign publications that it deems to have entered the realm of local politics.
27 Cheong (2013), p. 165.
28 Teo (2018).
29 Tan (2012).
30 Mano Sabnani (2017), pp. 158–9.
31 See Kuok (2016). An edited version of this story appears in Kuok (2017).

32 Interview with CNN's Fareed Zakaria at the SG50+ Conference, reported in *State Times Review* (2015).

33 Brooks (2014).

34 Wong (2015).

35 Cheng (2019).

36 *The Online Citizen* (2019).

37 Lam (2014).

38 Buettner (2017). Buettner has this to say about Singapore's status as one of the world's happiest countries: "Success for Singaporeans lies at the end of a well-defined path: Follow the rules, get into the right school, land the right job, and happiness is yours. . . . The people of Singapore today exemplify the third strand of happiness. You tend to be financially secure, have a high degree of status, and feel a sense of belonging." Sceptics were quick to note that the assessment was based not on people's expression of happiness, but on metrics related to good governance that enabled people to feel secure and satisfied with their living conditions and environment. Other assessments based on people's expressions of their own happiness level placed Singapore much further down international rankings. The 2018 World Happiness Report, for example, ranks Singapore in 34th place; see Helliwell, Layard and Sachs (2018).

39 In the World Happiness Index 2019, Singapore is ranked 34th. See Countryeconomy. com. (2019).

40 https://en.wikipedia.org/wiki/Singaporean_general_election,_2011. Retrieved 14 Dec 2017. See also Brown (2011).

41 Ibrahim and Lim (2003).

42 Tan Kin Lian (2017).

43 See Lianhe Zaobao (2019), cited in Lim (2019).

44 Singapore's population in 1965 was 1.89 million and 5.64 in 2018. See Trading Economics (2019), "Singapore Population," at https://tradingeconomics.com/singapore/population (22 February 2019).

45 Kuhn (1962, 1996).

46 In accordance with the new constitution, a candidate for the presidency in this election had to be an ethnic Malay. The only qualifying candidate was classified as Indian in her national registration identity card because her father was Indian. But she was deemed Malay for electoral purposes because she had been classified as a Malay candidate when she stood for election in her previous group representation constituency. Her adopted mother is Malay. She did not satisfy the financial expertise criterion, but qualified on another criterion, namely having been a Speaker of Parliament.

47 Of the two main parties, the Democrats and Republicans, neither is called "the Opposition" when the other party occupies power in the White House, the House of Representatives, or the Senate, or all of these. The notion of an opposition would be even more inappropriate if a third party emerges, as is increasingly likely given that traditional Republicans are abandoning the party in dismay after the rise of President Donald Trump.

References

Michael Barr. (2000). *Lee Kuan Yew: The Beliefs Behind the Man*. Washington, DC: Georgetown University Press.

Michael Barr. (2015). "Assess Lee Kuan Yew: Which One?" *New Mandala*, 25 March. Available online at www.newmandala.org/assess-lee-kuan-yew-which-one/. Accessed 25 December 2017.

Michael Billington. (1996). "Lee: 'The Best Bloody Englishman East of Suez'." *Executive Intelligence Review (EIR)* 23 (13), 22 March: 52–9. Available online at https://larouchepub.com/eiw/public/1996/eirv23n13-19960322/eirv23n13-19960322_052-britains_new_empire_strategy_inv.pdf. Accessed 14 April 2019.

David Brooks. (2014). "The Big Debate." *New York Times*, 19 May. Available online at www.nytimes.com/2014/05/20/opinion/brooks-the-big-debate.html. Accessed 14 April 2019.

Kevin Brown. (2011). "Singapore Opposition Makes Historic Gains." *Financial Times*, 8 May. Available online at www.ft.com/content/ac59d4aa-7924-11e0-b655-00144feabdc0. Accessed 14 December 2017.

Dan Buettner. (2017). "Blue Zones of Happiness: These Are the World's Happiest Places." *National Geographic*, November. Available online at www.nationalgeographic.com/magazine/2017/11/worlds-happiest-places/. Accessed 24th Dec 2017.

Chan Heng Chee. (1976). *The Politics of One-Party Dominance: The PAP at the Grassroots*. Singapore: University of Singapore Press.

Kenneth Cheng. (2019). "Going Beyond Consultations: Heng Wants to Cultivate Leaders in Every Corner of Society," *Today*, 5 May. Available online at www.todayonline.com/singapore/going-beyond-consultations-heng-wants-cultivate-leaders-every-corner-society. Accessed 29 May 2019.

Cheong Yip Seng. (2013). *OB Markers*. Singapore: Straits Times Press.

Chng Suan Tze, Low Yit Leng and Teo Soh Lung (2017). *1987: Singapore's Marxist Conspiracy 30 Years On*. Singapore: Function 8 Ltd.

Chua Beng Huat. (2002). *Communitarian Ideology and Democracy in Singapore*. London: Routledge.

Chua Beng Huat. (2017). *Liberalism Disavowed: Communitarianism and State Capitalism in Singapore*. Ithaca, NY: Cornell University Press.

Countryeconomy.com. (2019). "Singapore – World Happiness Index." Available online at https://countryeconomy.com/demography/world-happiness-index/singapore. Accessed 16 July 2019.

Derek Davies. (2015). "Lee Kuan Yew: Leader of Singapore Who Brought Wealth and Stability to the New State at the Cost of Personal Freedoms." *The Independent*, 23 March. Available online at www.independent.co.uk/news/people/news/lee-kuan-yew-leader-of-singapore-who-brought-wealth-and-stability-to-the-new-state-at-the-cost-of-10128809.html. Accessed 14 April 2019.

Ee Boon Lee and Lim Beng Tee. (1963). "Who's Who in the Big Round-Up." *Straits Times*, 6 February, p. 10. Available online at http://eresources.nlb.gov.sg/newspapers/Digitised/Article/straitstimes19630206-1.2.96. Accessed 14 April 2019.

Goh Chok Tong. (2002). "Speech by Prime Minister Goh Chok Tong at the Marine Parade National Day Dinner on Saturday, 24 August 2002, at 7.30pm at Roland Restaurant, Marine Parade Central." Singapore Government Press Release. Singapore: Media Relations Division, Ministry of Information, Communications and the Arts. Available online at www.nas.gov.sg/archivesonline/speeches/view-html?filename=2002082406.htm. Accessed 21 July 2019.

Han Fook Kwang, et al. (2011). *Lee Kuan Yew: Hard Truths to Keep Singapore Going*. Singapore: Straits Times Press.

John F. Helliwell, Richard Layard and Jeffrey D. Sachs. (2008). *World Happiness Report 2018*. New York: Sustainable Development Solutions Network. See http://worldhappiness.report/ed/2018/. Accessed 22 February 2019.

Lysa Hong, Poh Soo Kai and Tan Kok Fang (eds.). (2013). *The 1963 Operation Coldstore in Singapore, Commemorating 50 Years*. Petaling Jaya, Selangor and Kuala Lumpur: Malaysia Strategic Information and Research Development Centre, and Malaysia Pusat Sejarah Rakyat.

John Fuh-Sheng Hsieh (ed.). (2014). *Confucian Culture and Democracy*. New Jersey and London: World Scientific.

Zuraidah Ibrahim and Lydia Lim. (2003). "Lee Kuan Yew: This Is Who I Am." *Straits Times*, 14 September. Available online at www.straitstimes.com/singapore/lee-kuan-yew-this-is-who-i-am. Accessed 4 December 2017.

Jagjit Kaur. (2009). "Marxist Conspiracy." *Singapore Infopedia*. Singapore: National Library Board. Available online at http://eresources.nlb.gov.sg/infopedia/articles/SIP_1578_2009-10-31.html. Accessed 22 February 2019.

Kim Dae Jung. (1994). "Is Culture Destiny? The Myth of Asia's Anti-Democratic Values." *Foreign Affairs* 73 (6): 189–95. Available online at www.jstor.org/stable/20047005. Accessed 21 July 2019.

Thomas Kuhn. (1996) [1962]. *The Structure of Scientific Revolutions*, 3rd edition. University of Chicago Press.

Robert Kuok. (2016). "The Lee Kuan Yew They Knew: A Glimpse of His Human Side." *Straits Times*, 20 March. Available online at www.straitstimes.com/opinion/a-glimpse-of-his-human-side. Accessed 14 January 2018.

Robert Kuok. (2017). *Robert Kuok: A Memoir*. Singapore: Landmark Books.

Lam Peng Er. (2014). "The Politics of Confucianism and Asian Values in Singapore." In Hsieh John Fuh-Sheng (ed.), *Confucian Culture and Democracy*, 111–30. New Jersey and London: World Scientific.

Lee Kuan Yew. (1970). "The Twain Have Met." The Dillingham Lecture by the Prime Minister of Singapore, Wednesday, 11 November 1970. Singapore: Singapore National Archives, Document lky19701111. Available online at www.nas.gov.sg/archivesonline/data/pdfdoc/lky19701111.pdf. Accessed 21 July 2019.

Lee Kuan Yew. (1992). "Democracy, Human Rights and the Realities." Speech by Mr Lee Kuan Yew, Senior Minister of Singapore, at the Create 21 Asahi Forum on 10 Nov 92, Tokyo. Reproduced in *Speeches: A Bimonthly Selection of Ministerial Speeches*, Vol. 16, no. 6. Singapore: Ministry of Information and the Arts.

Lee Kuan Yew. (2007). "Speech by Mr Lee Kuan Yew, Minister Mentor, at the East Asian Institute's 10th Anniversary Lectures, 19th June 2007, 5.15pm at the Shangri-la Hotel." Singapore: Singapore Government Media Release. Available online at www.nas.gov.sg/archivesonline/speeches/view-html?filename=20070619989.htm. Accessed 19 February 2019.

Simon Leys (trans.). (1997). *The Analects of Confucius*. London and New York: WW Norton & Company.

Lianhe Zaobao. (2019). "社论：纠正过失恢复公众信心" [Editorial: Correcting Negligence to Restore Public Confidence], 1 February. Available online at www.zaobao.com.sg/zopinions/editorial/story20190201-928819. Accessed 23 February 2019.

Jonathan Lim. (2019). "Recent Major Lapses Involving Public Services May Be Result of a 'Muddling Along' Culture Taking Root." *Mothership.sg*, 2 February. Available online at https://mothership.sg/2019/02/zaobao-editorial-major-public-service-lapses/. Accessed 23 February 2019.

Lim Puay Ling. (2009). "Maintenance of Parents Act." *Singapore Infopedia*. Singapore: National Library Board. Available online at http://eresources.nlb.gov.sg/infopedia/articles/SIP_1614_2009-11-30.html. Accessed 20 February 2019.

Mano Sabnani. (2017). *Marbles, Mayhem and My Typewriter: The Unfadable Life of an Ordinary Man*. Singapore: Marshall Cavendish.

Mohammad Alami Musa. (2017). "Keeping Religion Separate From State." *Straits Times*, 14 December 2017. Available online at www.straitstimes.com/opinion/keeping-religion-separate-from-state. Accessed 12 May 2019.

Hussin Mutalib. (2004). *Parties and Politics: A Study of Opposition Parties and PAP in Singapore*. Singapore: Marshall Cavendish.

Matthias Nass. (2012). "The World According to Two Old Friends: Lee Kuan Yew and Helmut Schmidt." *Straits Times*, 22 September. Available online at www.straitstimes.com/singapore/the-world-according-to-two-old-friends-lee-kuan-yew-and-helmut-schmidt. Accessed 20 February 2019.

The Online Citizen. (2019). "Heng Swee Keat to Partner SGs to Design Policies for Peripheral Issues Instead of Pressing Ones," 15 June. Available online at www.theonlinecitizen. com/2019/06/15/heng-swee-keat-to-partner-sgs-to-design-policies-for-peripheral-issues-instead-of-pressing-ones/. Accessed 16 July 2019.

Klaus-Georg Riegel. (2000). "Inventing Asian Traditions: The Controversy Between Lee Kuan Yew and Kim Dae Jung." *Development and Society* 29 (1): 75–96. Available online at www.jstor.org/stable/deveandsoci.29.1.75. Accessed 21 July 2019.

Bilveer Singh. (2017). *Understanding Singapore Politics.* London: Imperial College Press.

States Times Review. (2015). "PM Lee Hsien Loong: Singapore Society Will Lose Out If Singaporeans Don't Have Aristocracy," 3 July. Available online at http://statestimesreview. com/2015/07/03/pm-lee-hsien-loong-singapore-society-will-lose-out-if-singaporeans-dont-have-aristocracy/. Accessed 24 December 2017.

Jeanette Tan. (2012). "Shock Therapy Economist Urges NWC to Call for More Wage Increases." *Yahoo Newsroom*, 25 October. Available online at https://sg.news.yahoo.com/-1-000-minimum-wage-scheme-as-%E2%80%98last-resort%E2%80%99-for-wage-shock-therapy – lim-chong-yah.html. Accessed 19 December 2017.

Tan Kin Lian. (2017). "Singapore Is Doomed Under PM Lee Hsien Loong." *TR Emeritus*, blog post, 22 December. Available online at www.tremeritus.com/2017/12/21/singapore-is-doomed-under-pm-lee-hsien-loong/. Accessed 23 February 2019.

Tan Tai Yong. (2019). "Crazy Rich Asians in Early Singapore's History." *Straits Times*, 26 February. Available online at www.straitstimes.com/opinion/crazy-rich-asians-in-early-singapores-history. Accessed 21 July 2019.

Teo You Yenn. (2018). *This Is What Income Inequality Looks Like.* Singapore: Ethos Books.

Thum Pingtjin. (2013). "The Fundamental Issue is Anti-Colonialism, Not Merger: Singapore's 'Progressive Left, Operation Coldstore, and the Creation of Malaysia." *Asia Research Institute, Working Paper Series*, no. 211. Singapore: Asia Research Institute, National University of Singapore.

Trading Economics. (2019). "Singapore Population." Available online at https://tradingeconomics. com/singapore/population. Accessed 22 February 2019.

Mary C. Turnbull (2009). *A History of Modern Singapore, 1819–2005: Revised edition*, 3rd edition. Singapore: Singapore University Press.

Ravi Velloor. (2015). "In Mr Lee Kuan Yew's Later Years, the World Turned to Him as Seer and Sage." *Straits Times*, 24 March. Available online at www.straitstimes.com/singapore/ in-mr-lee-kuan-yews-later-years-the-world-turned-to-him-as-seer-and-sage. Accessed 14 April 2019.

Geoff Wade. (2013). "Operation Coldstore: A Key Event in the Creation of Modern Singapore." In Lysa Hong, Poh Soo Kai, Tan Kok Fang (eds.), *The 1963 Operation Coldstore in Singapore, Commemorating 50 Years*, 15–72. Petaling Jaya, Selangor and Kuala Lumpur: Malaysia Strategic Information and Research Development Centre, and Malaysia Pusat Sejarah Rakyat.

Eleanor Wong. (2015). "Liberal Reflections on Loss and Acceptance in GE2015." *Straits Times*, 16 September. Available online at www.straitstimes.com/opinion/liberal-reflections-on-loss-and-acceptance-in-ge2015. Accessed 21 July 2019.

Fareed Zakaria. (1994). "Culture is Destiny: A Conversation with Lee Kuan Yew." *Foreign Affairs* 73 (2): 109–26. Available online at www.jstor.org/stable/20045923. Accessed 21 July 2019.

Zhang Zhibin (ed.). (2011). *Dynamics of the Singapore Success Story: Insights by Ngiam Tong Dow.* Singapore: Cengage Learning.

8

EAST ASIAN VALUES AND ECONOMIC GROWTH

Government leadership in a market economy is not only necessary but also desirable.
(Tu Wei-ming)[1]

Is economic growth determined by cultural values?

In a persuasive discourse on the Confucian qualities of East Asian economies accounting for their success, Tu Wei-ming considered key factors like the economic leadership role of the state and education as the "civil religion" of society.[2] These characteristics are clearly evident in countries like Japan, where a close relationship between the Ministry of Economy, Trade and Industry (METI) and the country's major corporations has been a longstanding tradition. Vogel was one of the earliest to make this observation.[3] Education has received heavy state emphasis particularly at the pre-university level, at which competition to enter a good university has traditionally been one the most critical challenges in the lifetime of an aspiring youth.

State economic leadership with vigorous state intervention in the market economy may also be observed in Taiwan and South Korea, particularly in early phases of development before these economies reached developed nation status. In South Korea, the concentration of financial and technology resources in large sprawling *chaebols* was guided by the heavy hand of the government eager to catch up with Japan after World War II. In Singapore, the existential crisis following her abrupt ejection from the Federation of Malaysian in 1965 facilitated ready acceptance of strong state intervention in the economy.

China's remarkable development since Deng Xiaoping's reforms in 1978 was achieved with active state control over the economy under a regime of benign authoritarian rule.[4] This has caused some Chinese observers to make a further assertion that authoritarian states deliver better growth than liberal democracies. Others make the more measured claim that the benevolent authoritarian governance of Confucian culture is the key factor for growth.

In reality, things are far from being that simple, as I shall argue in the following section.

Authoritarianism and economic growth

In a 1993 *Foreign Affairs* article that was later presented in a popular TED talk, Eric Li makes the assertion that China's economic performance has been attributable to her one-party system, in which leaders are chosen based on the systematic and rigorous application of meritocracy.[5] Meritocracy as practised in China implies that national leaders are not chosen through a popular vote as in liberal democracies, but rather through a rigorous evaluation process within the ruling party. It is an interesting thesis, somewhat sweeping in its claims, but certainly worth examining in detail.

Li likens the Organization Department of the Chinese Communist Party (CCP) to a giant human resources department continually selecting, training, and promoting cadres all the way up to the twenty-five-member Central Committee of the Politburo.

Each year, the government and its affiliates recruit university graduates into the civil service, state-owned enterprises, and government-linked social organizations. Recruits enter at the lowest *ke yuan* level and do not get promoted until they are reviewed a few years later by the Organization Department. They may then move up the ladder to more senior ranks: *fu ke* (副科), *ke* (科), *fu chu* (副处), and *chu* (处), in that order. The ablest rise to the elite *fu ju* (副局) and *ju* (局) levels, where they would typically manage areas with millions of people or companies with hundreds of millions of dollars in revenue.[6] In 2012, there were 900,000 officials at the *fu ke* and *ke* levels, 600,000 at the *fu chu* and *chu* levels, but only 40,000 at the *fu ju* and *ju* levels. After the *ju* level, a very talented few move up several more ranks to reach the Central Committee.

The journey takes two to three decades, and most of those who make it to the top would have gained managerial experience in just about every sector of Chinese society. Indeed, of the twenty-five Politburo members before the 18th Party Congress, nineteen had run provinces larger than most countries and ministries with budgets exceeding those of many governments. Xi Jinping took over thirty years to rise from a *fu ke* level deputy county chief in a poor village to party secretary of Shanghai and member of the Politburo. By the time he became president, Xi had governed areas with populations of over 150 million and a combined GDP of more than US$1.5 trillion.

This contrasts with the process within an electoral democracy like America, where popular appeal can catapult a first-term junior senator or a real estate billionaire with no public office experience to the presidency. Li speculates that "a person with Barack Obama's pre-presidential professional experience would not even be the manager of a small county in China's system."

Meritocracy had in fact been practised for centuries in imperial China through the *keju* (科举) imperial examination system. Any aspiring young scholar, rich or poor, could take the examinations to become a mandarin. If he performed well, he could rise quickly to the top. However, Li fails to mention that the imperial system was no guarantee against lax management and corruption, which was common under many bad emperors in history. Promotions were not always meritocratic as family connections and *guanxi*, not to mention palace intrigue, could also play a decisive role in important appointments and promotions. At best, one can only argue that meritocracy is a positive factor, but not a sufficient condition, for good governance.

Adaptability and legitimacy are offered by Li as the other two of three pillars of the Chinese state.

Despite its size, the party has been remarkably adaptable. It changed course several times over the last sixty years from land collectivization in the early 1950s and the Great Leap Forward of 1959 to farm privatization in the 1960s and market reforms beginning in 1978. In 2001, President Jiang Zeming opened up party membership to businessmen, greatly widening the party's talent pool.[7] Li praises the party's ability to quickly alter direction when mistakes were made, or when the economic landscape changed. This adaptability has been facilitated by the concentration of authoritarian power at the top where leaders can take decisive action without lengthy debates. Li, however, focusses on the bright side of the equation. Such concentration of power can and has led to major mistakes, such as the Cultural Revolution. But where strategies were in the right direction, authoritarian power would seem to have facilitated efficient and decisive implementation.

On the issue of the legitimacy of the government, Li argues that economic performance and social stability are better sources of legitimacy than the ballot box, as powerful interest groups can manipulate voters through the media. However, legitimacy can be undermined by performance failure; hence, the inherent instability of legitimacy. This could explain why China's leaders live in fear of an economic downturn. Constitutional reform to address this dilemma is the subject of intense debate among Chinese intellectuals today (more about this in the final chapter).

Li's arguments, though persuasive in explaining China's economic success of the last forty years, may be repudiated by failures under a similar system of governance in the first thirty years of CCP rule. At best, meritocracy administered with authoritarian governance may have been a key contributing factor, but it appears to be a less than a full and convincing explanation for contemporary China's economic success.

Human capital and growth

In a sharp critique of what he called the "Shanghai Theory of Economic Growth," economist Huang Yasheng characterizes Li's model of Chinese growth as one that gives credit to good infrastructure, strong government, and state capitalism with government ownership.[8] State capitalism and good infrastructure are associated with one-party authoritarian rule, which allows resources to be channelled expeditiously to where they are deemed to be needed. The implication of Li's model is that one-party rule avoids the failings of a liberal democracy where the government does not have a free hand to deploy resources in the most productive areas. Thomas Friedman's favourable comparison of China's gleaming infrastructure to America's creaky ones has been seen by Chinese writers as a vindication of the Chinese system.[9]

Huang selectively draws on telling statistics to dismiss Li's thesis that infrastructure provides the critical impetus to growth. The Soviet Union had far many more kilometres of telephone lines per capita than China, but grew at a much lower rate (see Figure 8.1). Likewise, India had a better system of railways than China, but has been outpaced by China in growth since the 1960s (Figure 8.2).

A comparison of Pakistan and India between 1990 and 2008 does not support the claim that authoritarianism is good for growth. Liberal democratic India's per capita GDP grew from $317 to $714, whilst authoritarian Pakistan with a large head start of $461 only grew to $650, trailing behind India (see Figure 8.2).

Which of These Two Countries Grew Faster?

- ☐ Telephones (1989):
  - Country 1: 107 telephone sets per 1,000 persons
  - Country 2: 10 telephone sets per 1,000 persons

- ☐ Length of railways (electrified railways)
  - Country 1 (1980–1981): 61,240 kilometres (5,345 kilometres)
  - Country 2 (1981): 53,900 kilometres (1,700 kilometres)

FIGURE 8.1 Better infrastructure does not ensure higher growth[10]

Note: The countries under "Telephones" are the Soviet Union (Country 1) and China (Country 2). The countries under "Length of railways" are India (Country 1) and China (Country 2).

A Tale of Two Asian Countries

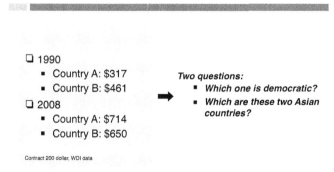

- ❏ 1990
  - Country A: $317
  - Country B: $461
- ❏ 2008
  - Country A: $714
  - Country B: $650

Two questions:
- *Which one is democratic?*
- *Which are these two Asian countries?*

Contract 200 dollar, WDI data

FIGURE 8.2 Liberal democratic India grew faster than authoritarian Pakistan[11]

Note: A is India, B is Pakistan. All amounts in US dollars.

The Power of Human Capital

❑ China's greatest advantage: Education

❑ Literacy rate (WDI 1990–1981 data)

■ Adult population: China 77.8%; India 48.2%

■ Women: China 68%; India 33.7%

❑ India is heavily focussed on tertiary education

■ Basic education is severely insufficient

FIGURE 8.3 Contrasting literacy rates in China and India[12]

But there appears to be a counter example when we compare China and India. In the thirty years up to 2010, India grew at half the rate of China. Was this a repudiation of liberal democracy for growth? Huang argues that the real underlying cause was not a difference in political system. Rather, it was the human capital gap between the two countries (see Figure 8.3).

China had a large lead in literacy rate in 1990. In fact, the literacy gap between the two countries was even wider. In China, literacy is defined as the ability to read and write 1,500 Chinese characters; but in India, it is the ability to write one's own name. Confucian emphasis on education in China had led to an enormous difference in the capabilities of the people of these countries to support development programmes. So significant was the difference in human capital that even during the ten chaotic years of the Cultural Revolution in China (1966–1976), when schools closed down and many workers were in the streets instead of their factories, China recorded a higher growth rate than India.

Huang further charges that Li himself seems to favour liberal democratic features like the growth of civil society to help deliver better services, a more independent media, and "intraparty democracy" for self-criticism and internal debate. These seem like steps towards a liberal democracy.[13]

Competing claims: a methodological assessment

Both Li and Huang make the same error, that of conflating correlation with causation. In Huang's case, although a higher human capital in China is a plausible contributing factor for her better growth rates compared to India's, social phenomena are almost never due to single-factor causes. In the 1950s, countries like Sri Lanka and Myanmar boasted higher educational levels than Singapore, and hence had an advantage in human capital. Yet they fell far behind in later years. One can say with some confidence that their lower educational levels today are the result rather than the cause of slower economic growth in the last five decades.

Determining causality is an age-old problem in the philosophy of science, and lies at the heart of disputes like the Li-Huang debate. Because of their complexity and the role of human actors, socio-economic theories cannot be tested with counterfactuals. We do not have the luxury of enacting scenarios such as this: what if India had an autocratic regime in the last thirty years? What if Deng had not burst on the scene in 1978 and introduced socialism with Chinese characteristics, injecting entrepreneurship and market while maintaining a tight rein over personal political freedoms? If post-Mao China had adopted Western capitalism and liberal democracy, would the country have grown even faster and with more long-term sustainability? One can only speculate about these matters as Li and Huang did, each driven by his own ideological commitments and biases that have been shaped by their personal experiences.

In experiments in the physical sciences, and to some extent in the biological sciences, it is possible to control causal factors with carefully designed scientific trials. The efficacy and safety of synthetic pharmaceuticals, for example, are put through randomized clinical trials in which the drug is given to one group and a placebo to another (the control group), and treatment outcomes are then compared. Such experiments are not usually possible for testing economic policies.

The Needham question and INUS conditions

The foregoing methodological issues are reminiscent of the infamous question posed by Cambridge sinologist Joseph Needham in the course of compiling the voluminous *Science and Civilisation in China*. Needham asked why China, which for centuries led the world in science and was pre-eminent for centuries in the Song dynasty, fell behind Europe after the Scientific Revolution in Europe in the sixteenth and seventeenth centuries, and stayed behind until very recent times. Why did the Scientific Revolution not happen in China?

Many scholarly treatises have been offered. These range from lack of creativity engendered by a rote learning Confucian culture and repressive bureaucratic administrations, to the difficulty of the Chinese written language that was ill-adapted to the expression of scientific ideas. Not surprisingly, none of them gives satisfactory explanations, as counterexamples could also be provided against each hypothesis.[14]

It was with cynical insight that Nathan Sivin dismissed the Needham question as a spurious paradox with a trite analogy: why did my name not appear on page 3 of today's newspaper? The answer is that the infinite host of factors leading to events occurring, or not occurring, can never be captured in a one cause explanation. It is futile to ask why something did not happen in history: "It belongs to an infinite set of questions that historians don't organize research programs around because they have no direct answers. They translate into questions about the rest of the world."[15]

It would be more useful to ask under what circumstances the Scientific Revolution took place in the seventeenth and eighteenth centuries in Western Europe, and observe the confluence of the myriads of circumstances leading to a certain historical event.

Sivin's argument falls within the ambit of the wider philosophical issue of the nature of causality. What does it mean for A to cause B? Significant things happen because of the confluence of many factors (i.e., "when the stars are aligned") that constitute the inexorable flow of historical events. Even trivial events happen by the same process, as the following example might illustrate.

Alfred Kinsey slipped on a banana peel on New York's Fifth Avenue and fell on top of a fashion model, Marilyn, ruining her face with an ugly scar and a black eye. Would it have made sense to dream up a sociological theory to explain the event? The event happened because there was a banana skin thrown by a careless boy walking on that same pavement minutes earlier. Other preconditions were required. The boy had to be in New York in that time period, and nobody before Alfred had slipped on the banana peel first. Other circumstances conspired to make the event happen. There was no heavy downpour prior to the event to wash the banana peel away. Mankind had to invent the automobile first so that streets were designed for cars and pavements for pedestrians. Alfred had to be born some forty years ago, and that required that his parents meet at a graduation ball two years earlier, and so on.

This line of argument was the subject of a seminal philosophical work by Mackie that introduced the concept of the "INUS condition" for the occurrence of an event. Mackie gave the example of a fire in a wooden house following an electric short circuit in the old wiring on one of the beams of the house. What caused the fire? It would be tempting to say that the cause was the short circuit that ignited the fire. But there had to be oxygen present for fire to burn, and the wood had to be dry enough. So oxygen and dry wood were also causal factors. One could also point to the poor quality of insulation. And of course, there would be no fire if the house had been built with steel instead of wooden beams. The dry climate caused wood to dry up and kindle easily.

The fire was caused by a *cluster* of factors, not just by the short circuit. In fact, the fire could have started without a short circuit, for example by extreme hot weather that ignited spontaneous combustion in the attic. Hence, a fire can be caused by *a number of* alternative clusters of factors.

In Mackie's example, the short circuit alone was insufficient to start a fire, but it was a part of this particular cluster of factors that, together, were sufficient to cause the fire (although other combination of factors could also have kindled the fire). The short circuit is called an "INUS condition," which is an acronym for Insufficient but Non-redundant part of an Unnecessary but Sufficient condition.[16] It was a philosopher's precise albeit tongue-twisting way of saying that *causes happen in clusters*. Furthermore, a particular event or phenomenon can be caused by any one of a number of possible clusters.

When this is applied to the Needham question, the search for *the* reason that a scientific revolution did not happen in China then becomes a misguided one. There is no single cause, neither is there a unique cluster of factors that would have dictated China's failure to have a scientific revolution. It did not happen because none of the clusters of factors came together to bring it about. It is not possible to identify what those clusters might be, nor would it be particularly useful. Suffice it to say, the conditions in Europe were different from those in China. We can now better appreciate Sivin's question as to why his name did not appear in this morning's papers.

Reviewing the Needham question in this light, it becomes clear that it is not only futile but basically misguided to seek out for a single reason for China's failure to have a scientific revolution. There is not even a unique set of conditions that must be present for it to occur.

If we apply Mackie's INUS conditions to explanations for high economic growth, it is evident that (1) there is no one single factor that is necessary and sufficient to bring about high growth; and (2) there can be several INUS conditions, each corresponding to one of several clusters of factors that could bring about growth. High growth occurred in China after Deng introduced liberalization reforms. These reforms may be viewed as an INUS condition, operating within a cluster of other factors that conceivably included (1) a high level of human capital from Confucian emphasis on education; (2) an authoritarian regime that facilitated effective implementation of economic policies and compliance by the people; and (3) a long tradition of business entrepreneurship. It certainly does not rule out other scenarios (clusters of factors) that could have brought about high growth. One such scenario might be a liberal democratic administration with enlightened and dedicated leaders, and a world trading environment favourable to China that she could exploit.

Japan achieved high growth for decades under a liberal democracy, high quality human capital, and a strong national will to rise from the ashes of war. It should serve as a reminder that alternative sets of conditions for economic success do exist.

Asian values

Claims about Asian values and strong leadership bringing prosperity overlook the complex nature of causality. Such claims are often proffered by those with biases toward certain forms of government, as illustrated by the sharp differences between Lee Kuan Yew and Kim Dae Jung described in the previous chapter of this book.

Cultural biases can lead even trained economists to unsound conclusions. In a *Foreign Affairs* article, Huang argued that democratic regimes provide better quality public services, basing his conclusion on the correlation between the level of democracy and the perceived quality of service, without taking into account other (confounding) factors that might affect service quality.[17] One only has to compare public services in India's liberal democracy with those in authoritarian Singapore to find a counterexample.[18]

When Angela Merkel asked why Germany, Europe's economic powerhouse, has never produced a Nobel laureate in economics, the reply from a cynical official was, "Mme Chancellor, if there were first-class economists, there would be no first-class economy."[19]

It is a sobering reminder of the limitations of economic doctrine in a world of human complexity.

Notes

1 Tu (1998).
2 Tu (1996a). See also Tu (ed.). (1996b), and Tu (1998).
3 Vogel (1979).
4 As explained in this book's Introduction and further argued in Chapter 9, "authoritarian" is used in a neutral non-pejorative sense to describe a style of governance that vests authority in a ruling group and places limitations on certain personal freedoms found in liberal democracies.
5 Li (2013b). See also Li (2013a).
6 *Fu* means deputy; *ke* is equivalent to a section head; *chu* is the level of a party secretary of a county city; and *ju* is at the level of a mayor of a prefectural city.
7 Pomfret (2001).
8 Huang (2011).
9 Friedman (2008).
10 Screenshot from Huang (2013).
11 Ibid.
12 Ibid.
13 Huang (2013).
14 A useful summary may be found in Mackerras (2018), pp. 21–35. See also Liu (2000).
15 Sivin (2005), p. 6.
16 Mackie (1974).
17 See Huang (2013), and Baum and Lake (2003).
18 More recently, Rizio and Sakali (2019), using regression analysis, found no significant correlation between autocratic regimes with economic growth. Nor could it make the claim that liberal democracies produce better growth rates.
19 Zhang (2011), p. 173, cited in Fukuyama and Zhang (2011).

References

Matthew A. Baum and David A. Lake. (2003). "The Political Economy of Growth: Democracy and Human Capital." *America Journal of Political Science* 47 (2): 333–47.

Thomas L. Friedman (2008). "A Biblical Seven Years." *New York Times*, 26 August. Available online at www.nytimes.com/2008/08/27/opinion/27friedman.html. Accessed 23 July 2019.

Francis Fukuyama and Zhang Weiwei. (2011). "Dialogue Between Francis Fukuyama and Zhang Weiwei." *New Perspectives Quarterly* 28 (4): 40–67. Available online at https://doi.org/10.1111/j.1540-5842.2011.01287.x. Accessed 21 July 2019.

Manuel Perez Garcia and Lucio De Sousa (eds.). (2018). *Global History and New Polycentric Approaches*. Singapore: Palgrave Macmillan.

Huang Yasheng. (2011). "Does Democracy Stifle Economic Growth?" Talk given at a TED Global Conference in July 2011. [Video file] Available online at www.ted.com/talks/yasheng_huang?language=en. Accessed 4 March 2019.

Huang Yasheng. (2013). "Democratize or Die: Why China's Communists Face Reform or Revolution." *Foreign Affairs* 92 (1): 47–54. Available online at www.foreignaffairs.com/articles/china/2012-12-03/democratize-or-die. Accessed 21 July 2019.

Eric X. Li. (2013a). "A Tale of Two Political Systems?" Talk given at a TED Global Conference on June 2013. [Video file] Available online at www.ted.com/talks/eric_x_li_a_tale_of_two_political_systems?language=en. Accessed 26 April 2019.

Eric X. Li. (2013b). "The Life of the Party: The Post-Democratic Future Begins in China." *Foreign Affairs* 92 (1): 34–46. Available online at www.jstor.org/stable/41721002. Accessed 21 July 2019.

Liu Dun. (2000). "A New Survey of the 'Needham Question'." *Studies in the History of Natural Sciences* 19 (4): 293–305. Available online at www1.ihns.ac.cn/members/liu/doc/needq.htm. Accessed 27 April 2019.

Colin Mackerras. (2018). "Global History, the Role of Scientific Discovery and the 'Needham Question': Europe and China in the Sixteenth to Nineteenth Centuries." In Manuel Perez Garcia and Lucio De Sousa (eds.), 2018, 21–35.

John L. Mackie. (1974). *The Cement of the Universe: A Study of Causation.* Oxford: Clarendon Press.

John Pomfret. (2001). "China Allows Its Capitalists To Join Party." *The Washington Post*, 2 July. Available online at www.washingtonpost.com/archive/politics/2001/07/02/china-allows-its-capitalists-to-join-party/98c51d3e-590c-4f1b-a52a-132b3def1281/?utm_term=.68c2a3b7fb6b. Accessed 3 March 2019.

Nathan Sivin. (1982). "Why the Scientific Revolution Did Not Take Place in China – Or Didn't it?" *Chinese Science* 5: 45–65. Revised version published 2005. Available online at www.sas.upenn.edu/~nsivin/from_ccat/scirev.pdf. Accessed 8 April 2019.

Stephanie M. Rizio and Ahmed Skali. (2019). "How Often Do Dictators Have Positive Economic Effects? Global Evidence, 1858–2010." *The Leadership Quarterly*. Amsterdam: Elsevier. Available online, dated 16th July 2019 www.journals.elsevier.com/the-leadership-quarterly/recent-articles. Accessed 22 July 2019.

Tu Wei-ming. (1996a). "Confucian Traditions in East Asian Modernity." *Bulletin of the American Academy of Arts and Sciences* 50 (2): 12–39. Available online at www.jstor.org/stable/3824246. Accessed 23 July 2019.

Tu Wei-ming (ed.). (1996b). *Confucian Traditions in East Asian Modernity: Moral Education and Economic Culture in Japan and the Four Mini-Dragons.* Cambridge, MA: Harvard University Press.

Tu Wei-ming. (1998). "East Asian Lecture Series: Asian Values and the Asian Economic Crisis." Speech at the Baker Institute, Rice University, 17 October. [Video file] Available online at www.youtube.com/watch?v=yLPJGb2zVRI. Accessed 28 February 2019.

Ezra Vogel. (1979). *Japan as Number One: Lessons for America.* Cambridge, MA: Harvard University Press.

Zhang Weiwei. (2012). *The China Wave: Rise of a Civilizational State.* Shanghai: World Century Publishing Company.

9

STATE GOVERNANCE IN CHINA AND EAST ASIA

Nothing turns out to be so oppressive and unjust as a feeble government.

(Edmund Burke)[1]

When Deng Xiaoping first employed catchy phrases like "socialism with Chinese characteristics" and "to get rich is glorious," there was a somewhat charming ring to these euphemisms for the calibrated adoption of ideas from the capitalistic market model.

Forty years on, China progresses towards becoming the world's largest economy and will increasingly rival the United States in international influence, military power, cyber technology, and the colonization of space. As a superpower with a large, highly educated middle class, the Marxist state governance model, originally adapted from the Soviets, will look increasingly anachronistic.

Of *Fortune*'s list of the world's 500 largest companies in 2018, China had 120 in the list, just behind the United States with 126, and ahead of Japan (which has 52). Three Chinese companies – State Grid, Sinopec, and China National Petroleum – occupied the second, third, and fourth spots on the list. China's big four banks were among the top ten most profitable.[2] China boasts the second highest number of billionaires in the world at 476, fast closing the gap with the United States at 585.[3]

Capitalistic institutions like the stock market and venture capital funds thrive in the country. Alibaba.com's initial public offering (IPO) at US$25 billion in September 2014 was the largest in world history, with the company's market capitalization at US$231 billion.

An increasing number of China's economists and policymakers hold Western graduate degrees, and, in a bid to move up university rankings, elite institutions such as Peking University and Tsinghua University have actively recruited Western academics

In the face of rapid changes to the economic system and financial regulation, and with hundreds of thousands of Chinese nationals returning each year with exposure to the Western capitalistic system, governance in China needs to move in step with the times. Can the so-called China Model endure?

The China Model

Extensively debated in the literature, the China Model has been touted as the answer to an increasingly dysfunctional Western democratic system exemplified by the disarray over the United Kingdom leaving the European Union (Brexit), the gridlock in the United States between the White House and Congress, and the leadership instability in Australia, which, in recent years, has seen an average of one new prime minister a year.

Although the China Model has been credited with China's rise, some may argue that success came *in spite of* rather than *because of* the model.[4]

The Fukuyama-Zhang debate

In a wide-ranging dialogue, American political scientist Francis Fukuyama debated the virtues and failings of the China Model with international relations professor Zhang Weiwei at Fudan University.[5] Even though Fukuyama, a scholar of democratic institutions, recently retracted his celebrated "end of history" claim that Western democracy had triumphed over all other political systems, he remains a firm believer in the superiority of Western democratic institutions over authoritarian systems.[6]

Fukuyama points out that the Chinese model depends on the integrity of leaders rather than on institutional safeguards, and professes greater faith in the hard power of institutions than in the soft power of moral imperatives. This stance reflects the inclination towards transparency and rigidity associated with a *yang* culture in which the rule of law is protected by institutions and procedures. In contrast, the Chinese have traditionally preferred the subtle and yielding *yin*, where moral judgment trumps rigid codes.

While conceding there is room for improvement in the rule of law in China, Zhang hastens to add that the United States has as much room for reform as China. In his view, there is much higher accountability in China. He cites the example of a recent fire in a residential building in Shanghai where twenty officials and business executives were punished once culpability was established. By contrast, when American citizens lost over one-fifth of their assets in the 2008 financial crisis, no financial regulator has yet been charged. On the contrary, some walked away with large financial windfalls.

But moral integrity fails when a bad authoritarian leader clings to power. This occurred during the Cultural Revolution, which wreaked havoc and destroyed countless lives. Zhang claims that China's political institutions have improved since then, and that there are now sufficient safeguards against this "bad emperor" problem. Today, no single leader can hold on to power without the support of senior party members. China's system of succession combines selection through proven performance in a meritocratic system. This "hybrid model" is superior to a complete reliance on elections practised in the West, which can and has often thrown up popular but incompetent leaders. Democracy, in Zhang's lexicon, exists in China in the form of extensive consultations among key players for important decisions. For the formulation of national five-year plans, thousands of rounds of discussions and consultations are held to reach a consensus. This stretches beyond the Western practice of democracy, and is an example of a "real democratic decision-making process."[7]

Ang puts it more cogently, arguing that the essence of the Chinese model was laid down by Deng Xiaoping, who did not blindly introduce Western-style democracy (I am reminded here of Gorbachev's failed *Perestroika* and *Glasnost*). Instead, he transformed the Chinese bureaucracy into a driver of economic growth by injecting "democratic characteristics into the bureaucracy, namely, accountability, competition, and partial limits on power."[8]

Fukuyama sees a lesser role for culture in a functioning political system. People's behaviour is determined more by the needs and aspirations of the current generation than the "weighty traditions" of the past. Although China is highly institutionalized and has checks and balances in its system, one cannot have confidence in the robustness of the system in the long run. This is because of the weakness in human nature to favour family and friends. In an oblique reference to *guanxi* relationships that have their roots in Confucian precepts of loyalty to family, clan, and bonds of brotherhood, he portrays the China system as one "without downward political accountability," making it difficult to prevent personal connections from creeping into the political system. While this is fair comment, Fukuyama may be disingenuous in suggesting that connections do not matter in Western democracies. How did so many Chicago friends of President Obama enter the White House, and are personal alliances not manifest in the Trump cabinet?

Fukuyama is optimistic that, with freedom of expression and genuine ability to debate, the West will "make the right decisions." Never mind that the West has not always made the right decisions.

In China, several millennia of a continuous culture can be expected to play a larger role in determining the political system than in most other countries. Zhang is confident that China's long cultural traditions will guide the middle class to support stability in the country, avoiding the destructive confrontations in Western politics. Zhang cites nineteenth-century conservative political philosopher Edmund Burke, who strenuously advocated that change in a political system can happen only within a country's traditions. But there is no assurance that culture can resist the disruptive process of social and economic changes in the long term. Three millennia of Chinese history and the relative stability of ruling dynasties can scarcely apply to the People's Republic born from a violent revolution, through which the emperor was replaced with the Chinese Communist Party (CCP) with no obvious mandate from heaven.

Zhang further contends that the current relationship between the middle class and the Chinese state is "positively interactive," and generates social cohesion in the Chinese society unmatched in Western society. While Westerners might view government as a "necessary evil," the Chinese view government as a "necessary virtue."[9]

Fukuyama and Zhang argue more from faith and ideological allegiance than from the weight of historical evidence. Western liberal democracies regularly fail, even within its short history of a few centuries. Chinese history is replete with instances of dynasties with a series of bad emperors.

Can China lead?

While it is reasonable to expect the political system not to run counter to culture, this alone is not enough. Checks and balances have to be in place, hence the need to build a constitution that both aligns with culture and embraces the universal values of accountability, transparency, space for responsible expression of ideas, and freedom from cruel repression.

Fault lines in Chinese society have developed since 1949. The worrying scenarios of conflict and resistance in Chinese society dramatized by Perry and Selden nine years ago have not disappeared; instead, they have apparently increased. This can only be expected from a more educated citizenry informed by travel, foreign education and access to the internet and social media.[10]

Prominent corporate figures have intimated unease with the tightening of control since Xi Jinping took over the helm in 2013 and launched a relentless campaign against corruption and, it has been alleged, his political rivals. There has also been harsher treatment of dissidents, tightening of restrictions on freedom against challenges the CCP's national policies, and the controversial elimination of a fixed term for the presidency. These trends raise the spectre of future challenges to the legitimacy of the CCP, popular demands for reform, and calls for a balance between personal freedoms and the efficacy of a benevolent authoritarian regime that inspires them to place communitarian values above the attractions of individual freedom.

Wearing their liberal democratic values on their sleeves, a group of senior academics from that bastion of Western capitalism, Harvard Business School, recently researched the contemporary Chinese corporate and social scene with help from former students now running enterprises in China.

Their conclusion was hardly surprising. Plagued by insecurity and paranoia over dissidence and foreign interference, China has the hardware, but presently lacks the software to lead the world.

> Why, one may ask, after decades of Chinese economic growth and now in a period of enduring economic crisis in the West, is the Chinese Party-State still so insecure? . . . China does not need the electoral democracy of the American in order to significantly increase honesty, transparency, and confidence in government and thus inspire trust. China's economy has leapt far ahead of its processes of governance. High-tech business parks coexist with low-tech surveillance and old-fashioned thuggery.[11]

The learned professors correctly observe that Chinese leaders have tightened their control over human rights, and there are indeed worrying signs of increased repressiveness. But there may be an underlying reason – an increased fear of political instability at a time when China's rise is viewed with hostility by the United States, and when the country needs to remain united against this new threat. Leaders like Xi remember only too well the chaos of the Cultural Revolution and the Tiananmen incident of 1989 when the country was on the verge of plunging into civil disorder. Chinese history teaches the good emperor that stability is to be prized above all. Dynastic change had always been too bloody, resulting in an unbearable toll on life and property.

The insecurity of the ruling elite stems also from the inadequacies of the Chinese constitution vis-a-vis the changing times, and by the perennial question of the legitimacy of the Communist Party.

To this burning issue, we must now turn.

Democracy and political legitimacy

There is a penchant in the West, particularly among right-wing journalists, to conflate democracy with political legitimacy. Calling a regime or a policy "undemocratic" is to say that it is unacceptable to reasonable men. The reality is that the West has hijacked the meaning of the word "democracy" and restricted its application to systems of government that resemble those in Western Europe and America where free elections are held and a political leader's tenure in office is subjected to the popular will.

The venerable Oxford Dictionary has a broader definition of democracy: "a form of government in which the people have a voice in the exercise of power, typically through elected representatives."[12] A claim can be made, contentious as it might be, that the Chinese political system is democratic. The people through the Communist party and the People's Congress have a voice in choosing their leaders and approving major policy changes. The fact that the president rules with an authoritarian style does not change the fact that he can be removed by elected representatives in the ruling Politburo. Zhang points out that in China's biggest national budget exercise, hundreds of thousands of discussions are held by a large number of people for the country's key five-year plans. These are people who have reached positions of power and influence through a meritocratic process.

The obsession among Chinese scholars to defend China's democratic credentials betrays a lack of confidence, perhaps even a sense of inferiority vis-à-vis the West. It has led some to claim that China is not just a true democracy, but also one that is clearly superior to liberal democracies in America and Europe.

I shall argue that China's brand of democracy and its legitimacy drew deeply from the cultural values that have permeated the language, folklore, rituals, and living habits of Chinese civilization for thousands of years. The cultural anchor of the Chinese people remains relatively stable and Confucian in character. It does not readily yield, not even to tidal changes in the economic landscape. In contemporary

Chinese society, children still seek parental approval for the choice of their spouses and filial piety remains largely intact. During the annual *Qingming* (tomb sweeping) Festival, hundreds of millions visit the graves of parents and ancestors, offering incense and gifts, and burning paper gold that their ancestors would enjoy in the other world.

Confucianism family, communitarian values, and respect for hierarchy and authority remain the dominant cultural traits of the Chinese. China's democracy, as it develops, must rest on these foundations.

"Democracy is a Good Thing"

In a much-cited controversial set of essays entitled "Democracy is Good Thing," an eloquent if solicitous case for the Chinese democracy was made by Yu Keping, Director of the Centre for Chinese Government Innovations at Peking University. Yu is familiar with Western thinking on democracy, having been a visiting scholar at the Brookings Institute and a fellow at the Harvard Kennedy School Ash Center for Democratic Governance and Innovation.[13]

Yu acknowledges that the standards expected of a Western democratic polity include a multi-party system, universal suffrage, and the separation of legislative, executive, and judiciary branches of government. Declining to abide by liberal Western usage of the term, his starting point is that the government's responsiveness to the needs and aspirations of its citizens is the fundamental criterion for a democracy. Democracy is a continuum rather than one side of a dichotomy. As long as a country has institutions to guarantee that government policies will reflect public opinion and enable citizens to participate in political life, and if the government is responsive to the interests of the people, it has a democratic system. China "can and should create a democratic model with Chinese characteristics" and develop democracy in line with the aspirations and culture of her people.

Instead of the contentious politics inherent in a multi-party system, Chinese polity already has in place "multi-party cooperation and political consultation under the leadership of the CCP." Checks and balances are maintained not by means of separate legislative, executive, and judicial bodies, but rather through the CCP's legislation, administration, and judiciary branches that enjoy some degree of independence from one another.[14]

Yu's proposal is tightly constrained by the overarching condition that the CCP runs the country, and that checks and balances must be contained within the Party. There is no institutional check on the CCP other than the will of the people, which can potentially challenge the Party's legitimacy should it fail to serve their needs and expectations. Such a challenge would amount to revolution.

Yu's proposals for Chinese democracy were collated in a recent volume, *Democracy in China: Challenge or Opportunity*. A review of the book in *The China Quarterly* criticizes Yu's "normative justifications for democracy" as simplistic and weak, and for being ambiguous about the practical features of democratic reform that resonate with Chinese cultural traditions. In particular, Yu fails to show how the system can avoid exploitation by a totalitarian ruling power.[15] However, it should be noted that Yu's proposal is a work in progress and awaits further research to flesh out details and supporting evidence.

Legitimacy and its discontents

The perennial question of the legitimacy of CCP rule is frequently singled out by international scholars as the Achilles heel of the Chinese state.[16] Most defenders of the Chinese model focus on pragmatic "performance legitimacy," by which the government retains support by ensuring security, economic growth, and an acceptable level of wealth distribution.[17]

Perry reminds us that performance legitimacy is not one of the three classical sources of legitimacy identified by nineteenth-century sociologist Max Weber.[18] Traditional legitimacy, as defined by Weber, was present in the imperial system from ancient times. This was replaced by "charismatic legitimacy" provided by Mao, who earned it through overthrowing the Nationalist (Kuomintang) regime.

It matters little that the Chinese government's legitimacy does not satisfy one or more of Weber's criteria. The appropriate question is whether performance can ensure political stability in the long run. Disappointing performance could lead to unrest. Chinese leaders in recent years have warned that a growth rate below 6 percent would lead to significant unemployment and social disorder. Failure to deliver is an ever-present risk, particularly if China's main trading partners, America and Europe, seek to contain China through trade tariffs and sanctions.

Performance-based legitimacy is inherently unstable. Poor performance, even if it is beyond the control of competent leaders, risks the country lapsing into its long tradition of regime change by civil war or revolution. Unrest that precipitates the fall of the CCP, with no party sufficiently organized to replace it, would be an unimaginable disaster. A more robust basis for legitimacy must remain a priority for the development of state governance in China.

Legitimacy can arguably be built on the broader and more forgiving basis of serving social justice, which the CCP can (and does) use as the moral rationale for its rule, as suggested by Perry.[19] In a sense, this harkens back to legitimacy derived from imperial times when the emperor's "Mandate of Heaven" prevailed only if the country was ruled justly and people's livelihoods were looked after. In modern times, security and social welfare for the masses continue be the most pragmatic and tangible result for claiming this mandate.

More importantly, this approach would be consonant with Confucian values and displace the foreign Marxist ideology incongruent with the culture and history of Chinese civilization. China has developed its own model and, today, only the internal administrative structure of the CCP remains partly faithful to the Soviet model. After Deng's reforms, Marxist ideology, even though it is still taught at universities and party schools, is hardly to be found in its unadulterated form within contemporary Chinese economic and social policies.

Meritocratic democracy

China has had a long history of rule by an authoritarian elite. This is unlikely to change in the foreseeable future. In contemporary China, the ruler's mandate from heaven has been replaced by support for the CCP from citizenry that live in security and enjoy welfare benefits under a meritocratic government, rigorous in rule by law, with the concentration of power in the top levels of the governance hierarchy.

One of the possible failings of the Western intellectual tradition is that freedom comes before most other needs. This observation has been made of Western society by philosopher Michael Sandel's popular work *Justice*. Justice based on virtue has yielded to justice based on freedom.[20]

It would appear that, in American society, unless you have a press as free as the *New York Times* and the BBC, the right to carry own guns, wide latitude to offend social norms in dress and conduct, and elected legislators free to engage in raucous debates with no conclusion, you do not have a *real* democracy.

Chinese scholars like Yu Keping have recast the concept of democracy more broadly to encompass benevolent authoritarian states that show accountability to the people through the provision of welfare, security, equality of economic opportunity, and fair treatment under the law. But they are up against the full weight of the Western media and intellectual establishment, who have decided how the term should be used.

China has two choices. She could consistently and vigorously describe her system of government as democratic, inventing an appropriate term for this kind of democracy in order to distinguish it from liberal democracy. Or she could desist from quibbling with the idle semantics of the West. Instead, she can employ scholars and spin doctors to invent a beautiful new term for her system of government and convince the world that it is a better system for China, if not for many other countries.

I propose that China describe herself as practising a form of *meritocratic democracy*, where meritocracy is the basis for the selection of the ruling elite, who are mandated to exercise some degree of authoritarian rule with wisdom and benevolence.

Because authoritarianism has acquired a pejorative meaning in Western usage, it is natural for most people to be repelled by the authoritarian inclination of a meritocratic democracy. I would suggest that we use the term "authoritarian" in a neutral sense, denoting a style of governance that favours "obedience to authority at the expense of personal freedoms."[21] The extent of restriction on personal freedoms can vary widely, from being softly benevolent as in Singapore where opposition parties are active and the online media is mostly anti-establishment, to being harsh in obedience enforcement as in China. It would depend on historical legacy and the nation's stage of economic and educational development. In each case, it represents a trade-off between personal freedoms and the discipline and efficacy that respect for authority can command.

A useful analogy can be drawn with governance in corporate America. Chief executives and boards of directors of these corporations manage their organizations by authoritarian rule. No elections are held for the appointment of executive management, and no referendums are needed for important corporate decisions. Authoritarianism can work well in capitalistic enterprises as an effective form of leadership, tempered no doubt by the need to show benevolence to employees and consideration for customers, suppliers, and the economic community at large.

China's democracy is still evolving. An historic opportunity awaits the Chinese leadership to develop a system of government that works for the long term without falling into the dysfunctional state of some Western liberal democracies. Importantly, it must also allow for sufficient personal freedoms that a more affluent and educated populace expects. Against this backdrop, bold proposals have been made for a reform of the Chinese constitution.

A Confucian constitution for China?

From the legendary days of revered founding emperors of the Chinese nation like Yao, Shun, and Huangdi, political legitimacy rested on a mandate from heaven. Guided later by philosophers of the Spring-Autumn period, particularly Confucianism, a formal imperial governance structure evolved that served the Chinese civilization as an unwritten constitution well up to the early twentieth century.

Admittedly, emperors sometimes lacked wisdom or would come under the influence of corrupt mandarins and eunuchs. Occasionally an emperor would be distracted by the charms of a concubine, as was the case of Emperor Tang Mingwang with Yang Guifei, resulting in his neglect of state matters, precipitating the decline of the Tang dynasty. But the robustness of the institutions of governance built on Confucian principles kept Chinese civilization intact.

Even conquests by the Mongols in the thirteenth century and the Manchus in the seventeenth century failed to shake the imperial system or weaken the sway that Confucian precepts held over state governance. Mongol rule collapsed in less than a century as the nomadic invaders failed to apply the lessons of the classics in governing the Chinese state. The Qing dynasty lasted much longer, over 250 years. Its longevity was enhanced by emperors schooled in the classics. The great Emperor Kangxi (1654–1722; Figure 9.1) was not only a soldier and political strategist, but also a scholar who compiled the first Chinese dictionary. He reputedly wrote questions and marked answers for the *keju* (科举) examinations that inducted the best scholars in the land into the imperial administration.

After the fall of the Qing dynasty, China experimented with different models of government in succession. To mobilize the masses for the overthrow of the decadent late Qing, the 1911 Xinhai Revolution led by Sun Yat-sen (Figure 9.2) acquired a veneer of Western democracy in the form of the "Three Principles of the People." This comprised *minzu* (民族), *minquan* (民权), and *minsheng* (民生). *Mingzu* advocated nationalism, *minquan* conferred power to the people to govern, and *minsheng* was Sun's version of economic welfarism, having, at its core, Confucian *ren* or benevolence with which a ruler treats his subjects.

FIGURE 9.1 The young Emperor Kangxi[22]

FIGURE 9.2 Sun Yat-sen, founder of the Republic[23]

The May Fourth Movement in 1919 yielded a fundamental change in the ideology of governance. Western liberal democratic ideas percolated in Chinese thinking through students who had studied in the West. Literacy was no longer the preserve of elite mandarins; there was now mass literacy and political consciousness. This laid the seeds for a continuing evolution of Chinese governance over the next hundred years, as Western ideas were selectively absorbed and adapted to Chinese culture.

After the Chinese Communist Revolution of 1949, a constitution was drawn up that essentially replaced the emperor with the CCP. Leaders are selected by party members through a largely meritocratic system, which produces an elite group in the form of the party's Politburo led by a seven-member Standing Committee headed by the president.

The humane authority constitution

Academics Jiang Qing and Daniel Bell forwarded a radical proposal for a new constitution for China in a 2012 essay in the *New York Times*. It avoided the Western liberal penchant for framing debates on the Chinese government's legitimacy in terms of democracy versus authoritarianism.

While democracy, in whatever form, seeks political legitimacy based solely on the sovereignty of the people – more specifically, a government that grants power to elected representatives – there is no compelling reason to have only one source of legitimacy, or for the Chinese government to seek any of the Weberian forms of legitimacy in Western history.

The authors pointed to defects in liberal democracy based on the will of electoral majorities. The will of the majority may be immoral – it can (and has often) expressed itself as racism, gun violence, cruel imperialism, and colonization. Short-term interests of powerful interest groups also often triumph over their own long-term good, as has happened in objections by the United States to measures to limit global warming.

Their proposal explicitly acknowledges China's Confucian heritage and calls for the institutionalization of her values by following the Confucian tradition of "humane authority" rather than Western-style multi-party elections in determining who governs. As proposed, humane authority appears at first blush to have the check and balance form of the American constitution, which has three branches of government – the executive, the legislature, and the judiciary. But the similarity ends there.

As first propounded, the terms used to describe these branches of government sound almost bizarre to a Western audience:

> In modern China, Humane Authority should be exercised by a tricameral legislature: *a House of Exemplary Persons* that represents sacred legitimacy; *a House of the Nation* that represents historical and cultural legitimacy; and *a House of the People* that represents popular legitimacy. The leader of the House of Exemplary Persons should be a great scholar . . . nominated by scholars and examined on their knowledge of the Confucian classics and then assessed through . . .

progressively greater administrative responsibilities. The leader of the House of the Nation should be a direct descendant of Confucius; other members would be selected from descendants of great sages and rulers, along with representatives of China's major religions. Finally, members of the House of the People should be elected either by popular vote or as heads of occupational groups.[24]

The essay predictably sparked a torrent of criticism. A more perceptive and measured critic identified its principal weakness as betraying "popular sovereignty," by which the masses have a say about who rules the country: "When the Qing dynasty finally fell in 1911, China embraced the notion of popular sovereignty, and it has never relinquished that position. . . . Giving the 'people' only one house, which could be blocked and legislatively defeated by the other two elitist houses . . . would not be a return to an ideal Chinese past. It would more likely spark a popular revolution."[25]

The proposals were met with guarded sympathy by some Chinese scholars, but faced heavy criticism by Chinese compatriots in the mainland and Hong Kong. A subsequent book edited by Bell stated Jiang's views in greater detail, backed by historical references and philosophical reasoning. *A Confucian Constitutional Order: How China's Past Can Shape its Political Future*, as a political roadmap for constitutional reform, received mainly negative reviews in Western critics, whilst observers in China and Hong Kong found useful ideas in it.[26] Most conceded his overarching point: that the constitution for China must in some way incorporate its cultural values, and much of that is Confucian in character.[27] Asian scholars were more sympathetic, although Li Chenyang from Singapore preferred a Confucian society that chooses its political leaders by elections. Joseph Chan of the University of Hong Kong acknowledged that Confucianism can positively shape political institutions, but prefers not to overtly embed Confucianism in the constitution.[28]

As Bell points out, Jiang's book is a work of "political imagination" that is open to modifications and radical reworking. In a subsequent book, Bell argues cogently for a "vertical democratic meritocracy" with political meritocracy at the top and democracy at the bottom.[29] It does away with institutional democracy at the top, allowing instead the meritocratic process and proven track records to deliver talented people to leadership positions.

The practice of political meritocracy has for millennia been an essential part of Chinese political culture and China. Jiang and Bell have in fact forcefully argued that it cannot be omitted from future constitutional reform. The Chinese model of governance awaits a national constitution more in keeping with the twenty-first century. Such a constitution would be built on Confucian traditions, and the rule of an elite selected through a disciplined and transparent meritocratic process.

Such a system may not export well to Western Europe and America with their markedly different histories and cultures that place a much higher emphasis on personal freedoms than Eastern Confucian societies. But it may offer useful ideas at a time when many in the Western world have doubts about liberal democracy in which divergent interests prevent consensus vis-a-vis the pursuit of wise long-term policies.

Patrick Deneen's recent influential book *Why Liberalism Failed* argues that liberalism has betrayed its promises of fostering equality and giving average people control over government; instead, inequality has increased and a new aristocracy exerts political influence, alienating average people from the government. In effect, Deneen argues that liberalism today has forsaken its roots in ancient Greece, and detached people from tradition and community. In that sense, it is anti-culture:

> By ancient understandings, liberty was the condition of self-governance – requiring an extensive habituation in virtue, particularly self-command and self-discipline. . . . The achievement of liberty required constraints upon individual choice. This limitation was achieved . . . through extensive social norms in the form of custom. . . . Liberalism (today) reconceives liberty as the opposite of this older conception. It is understood to be the greatest possible freedom from external constraints, including customary norms.[30]

Under the influence of philosophers like Locke, the men who founded the new liberal ideology placed the individual at the centre. They distrusted a system of government based on virtue and, instead, based it on enlightened self-interest. Viewing it from the point of East Asian governance, liberty in ancient Greece – like Confucian governance – was rooted in virtue and community values; but today, it is centred on the individual.

David Brooks of the *New York Times* has similar misgivings about liberal democracies run by leaders chosen via electoral popularity. Writing on the occasion of the passing of Singapore's founding Premier Lee Kuan Yew in 2015, Brooks opined that some variant of the Singapore meritocratic model may well be what the West needs to fix its ailing democratic system. The problems of American democracy, he conjectured, could perhaps be tackled by becoming "less democratic" in leadership selection at the national level so as to become more democratic at the local level.[31]

It would be an ironic twist in the history of political thought if the Chinese meritocratic democracy model, with suitable adaptation to Western culture and history, provided the intellectual leads for political and constitutional reform in the West. Such reform could yield a system that is less troubled by internal tensions and enjoy more support from the common man. As Burke put it, "Nothing turns out to be so oppressive and unjust as a feeble government." There could come a time when people rise up against excessive freedoms that have become oppressive by the ineffective and unjust governance it engenders.

Conclusions

Would the meritocratic democratic model work in other East Asian countries and, indeed, other nations in Asia, Africa, and South America?

The new democracies of Myanmar and Vietnam are suitable candidates for such a democracy. Vietnam has Confucian roots, and her governance model could well transform to an authoritarian democracy. Myanmar lived under authoritarian rule for over seven decades under a military dictatorship and is struggling with a hybrid model of a liberal democracy held in check by the military. Constitutional reform may lead to benevolent authoritarianism with adequate means to remove a bad leader. North Korea will likely switch to the China Model when the dynastic grip of the Kim family finally loosens.

In Southeast Asia, Indonesia, Thailand, and the Philippines are messy democracies with an unsavoury mixture of liberal democratic institutions and authoritarian leaderships. Of these, Thailand is arguably the most complex as Western-style democratic institutions appear to be failing. The country went through a bruising and confusing general election in 2019, with the outcome pre-empted by the votes of senators chosen by the military. The king and the army *de facto* hold all the levers of power, and are able to circumvent the popular mandate expressed through the electoral process. There is an arguable case for transforming the current system into a meritocratic democracy with a moderate touch of authoritarian governance.

The Singapore model is a softer form of meritocratic democracy than China's. It delivers economic growth, safe streets, and efficient public services with a low level of corruption. Although governance was originally built on liberal democratic institutions, the dominant ruling party has over the last sixty years acquired an iron grip on power that enables it to practise benign authoritarian governance while continuing to enjoy electoral support. The government makes tough long-term decisions, sometimes over the objections of the general public, with the confidence of staying in power. However, with the passing of her founding father Lee Kuan Yew, the governance model may see a paradigm shift in line with the emergent cultures of the Millennial and Z Generations and the rising influence of Western liberalism.

In the longer term, similar paradigm shifts may well sweep China and other Asian countries. But if history is any guide, these shifts will not contravene the enduring principle that each nation's own culture must serve as the foundation for her system of governance.

Culture rules governance. To violate this principle is to ignore the lessons of history.

Notes

1 *Goodreads.* www.goodreads.com/quotes/268677-nothing-turns-out-to-be-so-oppressive-and-unjust-as. Accessed 22 July 2019.
2 Zhang (2017).
3 Dou (2018); Yancey-Bragg (2018).
4 Huang (2013).
5 Fukuyama and Zhang (2011).
6 Fukuyama (1989, 2014).
7 Zhang (2011), p. 158.
8 Ang (2018). See also her Camden Conference talk (2019) at https://youtu.be/2_bNB4S_HTw (accessed 18 July 2019).
9 Zhang (2011), p. 129.
10 See Perry and Selden (2010) and Zang (2011).

11 See Abrami, Kirby and McFarlan (2014), Chapter 7, section titled "Can China lead?"
12 See Soanes' and Stevenson's (2008) entry on "Democracy" (2008).
13 Yu (2009).
14 Yu (n.d.). Similar content may be found in Yu (2016).
15 Jia (2017), pp. 1119–21.
16 Perry (2018), pp. 11–17.
17 See, for example, Li (2013); Yu (2016); Zhu (2011), p. 134.
18 Max Weber identified three basic sources of regime legitimacy: traditional, charismatic, and rational-legal. The CCP does not currently fit into any of these. Traditional legitimacy in the form of dynastic rule of emperors fell in 1911; Mao's charismatic rule has passed; and the CCP currently holds power by the perpetuation of its ascendancy following the civil war that ended in 1949, rather than being conferred power by rule of law (cf. Weber's rational-legal source of legitimacy).
19 Perry (2018).
20 Sandel (2010), p. 9.
21 See Soanes' and Stevenson's (2008) entry on "Authoritarianism" (2008).
22 Picture from https://commons.wikimedia.org/wiki/File:Young_Kangxi.jpg.
23 Picture from https://commons.wikimedia.org/wiki/File:Sunyatsen1.jpg.
24 Jiang and Bell (2012).
25 Crane (2012).
26 Jiang (2013).
27 Minzer (2013) and Angle (2014).
28 Their comments are in Bell (2015).
29 Bell (2015).
30 See Deneen (2018), Preface.
31 Brooks (2014).

References

Regina Abrami, William Kirby and Warren McFarlan. (2014). *Can China Lead? Reaching the Limits of Power and Growth*. Cambridge, MA: Harvard Business Review Press.

Ang Yuen Yuen. (2018). "Autocracy With Chinese Characteristics: Beijing's Behind-the-Scenes Reforms." *Foreign Affairs* 97 (3): 39–46. Available online at https://sites.lsa.umich.edu/yy-ang/wp-content/uploads/sites/427/2018/04/YYA_FA_Chinas-behind-the-scenes-reforms-final.pdf. Accessed 18 July 2019.

Ang Yuen Yuen. (2019). "How the West (and Beijing) Got China Wrong." Talk given at the 2019 Camden Conference on "Is This China's Century?" [Video file]. Available online at https://youtu.be/2_bNB4S_HTw. Accessed 18 July 2019.

Stephen C. Angle (2014). "A Confucian Constitutional Order: How China's Ancient Past Can Shape Its Political Future by Jiang Qing, translated by Edmund Ryden, edited by Daniel A. Bell and Ruiping Fan (review)." *Philosophy East and West* 64 (2): 502–6. Available online at https://doi.org/10.1353/pew.2014.0020. Accessed 18 July 2019.

Daniel A. Bell (2015). *The China Model: Political Meritocracy and the Limits of Democracy*. Princeton, NJ: Princeton University Press.

David Brooks. (2014). "The Big Debate." *New York Times*, 19 May. Available online at www.nytimes.com/2014/05/20/opinion/brooks-the-big-debate.html. Accessed 14 April 2019.

Sam Crane. (2012). "A Confucian Constitution for China: Where's the Popular Sovereignty?" [Blog post]. *The Useless Tree*, 11 July. Available online at https://uselesstree.typepad.com/useless_tree/2012/07/a-confucian-constitution-for-china-wheres-the-popular-sovereignty.html. Accessed 30 March 2019.

Patrick J. Deneen. (2018). *Why Liberalism Failed*. New Haven, CT: Yale University Press.

Dou Shicong. (2018). "Pony Ma Moves to Top Spot to Become Richest Chinese on Forbes 2018 List of Billionaires." *Yicai Global*, 7 March. Available online at www.yicaiglobal.com/news/pony-ma-moves-to-top-spot-to-become-richest-chinese-on-forbes-2018-list-of-billionaires. Accessed 16 June 2019.

Francis Fukuyama. (1989). "The End of History?" *The National Interest*, 16 (Summer): 3–18. Available online at www.jstor.org/stable/24027184. Accessed 21 July 19

Francis Fukuyama. (2014). *Political Order and Political Decay: From the Industrial Revolution to the Present Day*. New York: Farrar, Straus and Giroux.

Francis Fukuyama and Zhang Weiwei. (2011). "Dialogue Between Francis Fukuyama and Zhang Weiwei." *New Perspectives Quarterly* 28 (4): 40–67. Available online at https://doi.org/10.1111/j.1540-5842.2011.01287.x. Accessed 21 July 2019.

Huang Yasheng. (2013). "Democratize or Die: Why China's Communists Face Reform or Revolution." *Foreign Affairs* 92 (1): 47–54. Available online at www.foreignaffairs.com/articles/china/2012-12-03/democratize-or-die. Accessed 21 July 2019.

Jia Peitao. (2017). "Book review of *Democracy in China: Challenge or Opportunity*, by Yu Keping Hackensack, NJ: World Scientific Publishing, 2016 vi + 235 pp. £95.00 ISBN 978-981-4641-52-4." *The China Quarterly* 232 (December): 1119–21. Available online at https://doi.org/10.1017/S030574101700145X. Accessed 21 July 2019.

Jiang Qing. (2013). *A Confucian Constitutional Order: How China's Past Can Shape its Political Future*. Translated by Edmund Ryden, edited by Daniel A. Bell and Ruiping Fan. Princeton, NJ: Princeton University Press.

Jiang Qing and Daniel A. Bell. (2012). "A Confucian Constitution for China." *New York Times*, 10 July. Available online at www.nytimes.com/2012/07/11/opinion/a-confucian-constitution-in-china.html. Accessed 30 March 2019.

Li Chenyang. (2012). "Equality and Inequality in Confucianism." *Dao: A Journal of Comparative Philosophy* 11 (3): 295–313. Available online at https://doi.org/10.1007/s11712-012-9283-0. Accessed 21 July 2019.

Eric X. Li. (2013). "The Life of the Party: The Post-Democratic Future Begins in China." *Foreign Affairs* 92 (1): 34–46. Available online at www.jstor.org/stable/41721002. Accessed 21 July 2019.

Carl Minzer. (2013). "Book review of *A Confucian Constitutional Order: How China's Ancient Past Can Shape Its Political Future*. By Jiang Qing, Translated by Edmund Ryden; Edited by Daniel Bell and Ruiping Fan. Princeton and Oxford: Princeton University Press, 2013. vi + 256 pp. $39.50; £27.95. ISBN 978-0-691-15460-2." *China Quarterly* 215: 767–9. Available online at https://doi.org/10.1017/S0305741013000829. Accessed 21 July 2019.

Elizabeth J. Perry. (2018). "Is the Chinese Communist Regime Legitimate?" In Jennifer Rudolph and Michael Szonyi (eds.), *The China Questions: Critical Insights into a Rising Power*, 11–17. Cambridge, MA: Harvard University Press.

Elizabeth J. Perry. and Mark Selden. (2010). *Chinese Society: Change, Conflict and Resistance*, 3rd edition. Oxon and New York: Routledge

Jennifer Rudolph and Michael Szonyi (eds.). (2018). *The China Questions: Critical Insights into a Rising Power*. Cambridge, MA: Harvard University Press.

Michael Sandel. (2010). *Justice: What's The Right Thing to Do?* London: Penguin Books.

Catherine Soanes and Angus Stevenson. (2008). "Authoritarianism." In *Concise Oxford English Dictionary*, 11th edition. Oxford: Oxford University Press.

Catherine Soanes and Angus Stevenson. (2008). "Democracy." In *Concise Oxford English Dictionary*, 11th edition. Oxford: Oxford University Press.

N'dea Yancey-Bragg. (2018). "Jeff Bezos Unseats Bill Gates on Forbes 2018 Richest Billionaires List." *USA Today*, 6 March. Available online at www.usatoday.com/story/money/2018/03/06/jeff-bezos-unseats-bill-gates-forbes-2018-richest-billionaires-list/398877002/. Accessed 16 June 2019.

Yu Keping. (n.d.). "Democracy in China: Challenge or Opportunity?" [Monograph] Cambridge, MA: Harvard Kennedy School Ash Centre. Available online at https://ash.harvard.edu/files/ash/files/democracyinchina_0.pdf. Accessed 9 May 2019.

Yu Keping. (2009). *Democracy Is a Good Thing*. Washington, DC: Brookings Institution Press.

Yu Keping. (2016). *Democracy in China: Challenge or Opportunity?* Hackensack, NJ: World Scientific.

Zang Xiaowei. (2011). *Understanding Chinese Society*. Oxon and New York: Routledge.

Zhang Jie. (2017). "Global 500: Chinese Companies Race Ahead." *China Daily*, 20 July. Available online at www.chinadaily.com.cn/a/201807/20/WS5b518b77a310796df4df7b77.html. Accessed 21 July 2019.

Zhang Weiwei. (2012). *The China Wave: Rise of a Civilizational State*. Shanghai: Century World Publishing Company.

Zhu Yuchao. (2011). "'Performance Legitimacy' and China's Political Adaptation Strategy." *Journal of Chinese Political Science* 16 (2): 123–40. Available online at https://doi.org/10.1007/s11366-011-9140-8. Accessed 21 July 2019.

EPILOGUE

Yin-yang and the Thucydides trap

Culture and the Thucydides's Trap

In his classic *The United States and China,* John Fairbank gave us a glimpse of the immensely complex love-hate relationship between the United States and China, one that defies simple portrayal as a Huntingtonian clash of civilizations or a case of great power rivalry.[1] After "America-first" President Donald Trump burst onto the international scene, Graham Allison raised the spectre of the Thucydides's Trap and the inexorable march to war between China and the United States.[2] This frightening prospect evokes memories of war between Athens and Sparta of ancient Greece, Britain and France in the 18th century, Japan and Russia in the late Meiji era, and the Cuban missile crisis that brought the world to the brink of annihilation.

But development of nuclear weapons has made all-out war unlikely between major powers for the simple reason that it would only lead to total mutual destruction. Instead, a trade war broke out after Trump seized the American presidency on a wave of popular discontent among lower-income Americans whose livelihoods he claimed had been damaged by loss of manufacturing jobs to China. He contended also that China engaged in unfair trade practices and currency manipulation. The trade war is but a cover for a wider conflict on many fronts – technological leadership, control of financial markets, military superiority, and soft power over developing nations. At stake is nothing less than the continued viability of the US economy, which has become dependent on a mountain of debt built on the US dollar as the main trading and reserve currency of the world. Technological leadership spawned great American internet companies like Amazon, Apple, Facebook, Google and Microsoft, as well as aerospace giants like Boeing, Lockheed, and Pratt and Whitney. This is being challenged by China's Alibaba, Huawei, Tencent, and a fast-growing list of companies offering advanced technology ranging from high-speed rail transportation to artificial intelligence.

American nationalism has revived paranoia over a new "yellow peril" that allegedly robs honest, hardworking Americans of a decent living, impelling opposite ends of the political spectrum to close ranks against China's further rise. Even the prominent Texas senator and one-time Trump rival for the presidency Ted Cruz lapsed into near hysteria over this imagined threat to Western civilization.[3] Wang Gungwu's timely review of Chinese history describes the current scenario incisively:

> "To the Westerner, it was (historically) inconceivable that the Chinese would do anything except learn from them. . . China was no threat to the liberal ideas and institutions that made the world civilized. Today that picture of the norm is being challenged. A new scenario is unfolding as "America first" takes centre-stage. . . Xi Jinping and his colleagues are not so foolish to try to replace the United States as a dominant force. Newly rising powers like China and India could at best hope that a multi-polar order will be a better foundation for a durable peace. If they could persuade a less confident American superpower that multi-polarity would guarantee America's place in world affairs, there should be no need for alarm. If they fail, the defensive superpower would refuse to accept a lesser hegemony."[4]

Over the long term, this new cold war would destroy an enormous amount of economic value in the world and could cripple the liberal world order that the United States—in her wisdom—had played a major role in creating, an order that has been the framework for unparalleled advances in global prosperity in the last seven decades.

Is Thucydides's Trap inevitable? Will the new cold war be the greatest destroyer of economic value that the modern world has ever seen?

In this deeply worrying context, the theme of this book, that culture rules governance, is particularly relevant. Thucydides's Trap can be averted by espousing the principle of *yin* and *yang*, and the wisdom of balancing these two forces. Each acts as both a restraint and supporter of the other. As we saw in Chapter Four of this book, an excess of either *yin* and or *yang* is inimical to the welfare of any system, be it that of human physiology or the liberal order of world trade, investment and sharing of knowledge.

America and much of the Western world is *yang* in nature, steeped in the culture of wide personal freedoms, transparent rules of governance, and impatience for quick solutions to problems. The East, exemplified by China, is *yin*. It prizes communitarian welfare over individual freedom and is able to accept and thrive under benevolent authoritarian rule. It makes a virtue of flexibility, is less governed by rigid rules than by moral precepts, and has the patience to wait—many decades if necessary—to achieve strategic goals.

These represent different values and political and social ideologies. There is no necessity, neither is it desirable, for either *yin* or *yang* to dominate or prevail. Without the support and restraining influence of the other, the system will eventually falter, as America might have begun to in the last two decades. This is the core aspect of the *yin-yang* balance. It is the reason why China has repeatedly declared that she has no wish to export her system of governance, or tolerate any preaching on the virtues of liberal democracy that have no roots in China, and likely never will.

The sensible solution is for China and the US to coexist, compete fairly with each other, and cooperate when it benefits both sides as well as the rest of the world. The mutual balancing restraint of *yin* and *yang* can take many positive forms, with China and the US each playing their part in a constructive way.

America could continue to prevail on China to engage in fairer trade practices, and to rigorously pursue the protection of intellectual property rights. She could use moral suasion on China to show greater tolerance for well-meaning dissidents whose aim is not to undermine the ruling Communist party, but to make it more responsive to the wish for more freedom of choice. She can use her influence on Southeast Asian nations to resolve territorial claims in the South China Sea through peaceful negotiations.

On China's part, her ability to pull the country together for a common good can be an example to America, whose raucous congressional proceedings and rambunctious media may be fun for foreigners to behold, but sadly chip away at America's greatness. China's international influence can moderate American penchant to trample on the sovereignty of other nation-states through means such as the promotion of regime change. She can call out American recalcitrance over global issues such as the abandonment of the Paris Climate Change Accord. In business rivalry, China's leapfrogging over America in areas like 5G communication, supercomputing and space satellite launches can only be salutary to America's resolve to stay fighting fit for competition.

Sustained conflict with the aim of destroying one's opponent is foolish and unenlightened, and can only lead to mutual decline. To borrow an analogy from naturalistic Chinese medicine, it is unhealthy for the human body when either *yin* or *yang* is weak, and the other becomes dominant. These imbalances create internal pathologies, disrupt natural flows in the body, and upset homeostasis. Chinese medical therapies consist of balancing *yin* and *yang* forces in the body. This profound insight has reputedly brought healing and good health to untold millions through the ages.

Yin-yang terminology may sound esoteric to the West, but its underlying rationale is universal and certainly not alien to Western culture. *Yin-yang* balance is closely allied to the concept of checks and balances in governance. Healthy contention between *yin* and *yang* underlies the virtue of business competition, keeping each party alert and nimble.

For China and the United States to ignore this wisdom is to imperil the world, and destroy the liberal world order that past world leaders and the forebears of Trump have painstakingly built for mankind.

Notes

1 Fairbank (1983).
2 Allison (2018).
3 Gertz (2019).
4 Wang (2019), pp. 33–34.

References

Graham Allison. (2018). *Destined for War: Can America and China Escape Thucydides's Trap?* Boston, MA: Mariner Books.

John K. Fairbank. (1983). *The United States and China*, 4th ed. Cambridge, MA: Harvard University Press.

Bill Gertz. (2019). "Cruz on China threat." *Washington Post*, 10 April. Available online at https://www.washingtontimes.com/news/2019/apr/10/ted-cruz-says-china-is-greatest-us-threat/. Accessed 26 September 2019.

Wang Gungwu. (2019). *China Reconnects: Joining a Deep-rooted Past to a New World Order.* Singapore: World Scientific.

INDEX

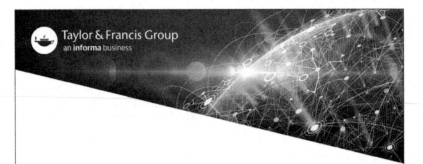

Printed in the United States
by Baker & Taylor Publisher Services